A IS FOR ADVENT

IS FOR
ADVENT

charles w. ferguson

LITTLE, BROWN AND COMPANY · BOSTON · TORONTO

LIBRARY OF CONGRESS CATALOG CARD NO. 68-30879

FIRST EDITION

The stanza from the poem "Miracles" on page 71 is reprinted from
New magazine, July, 1967, by permission of the magazine and of
its author, Robert Tree West.
© 1967 by Unity School of Christianity.

Published simultaneously in Canada

by Little, Brown & Company (Canada) Limited

PRINTED IN THE UNITED STATES OF AMERICA

PLEASE!

Time was when, if someone had called you a dunce, it would have been a compliment. The spelling was different, but dunses were once esteemed as very bright fellows. The name came from a Scottish theologian, John Duns Scotus. He was known as the Subtle Doctor because he could spin fine theories with a nimble tongue, and his followers were Dunsmen or Dunses. They enjoyed great fame in carrying on the Doctor's work after he died in 1308.

Then the climate of religious opinion changed. Within two hundred years after his death, the name of John Duns Scotus had fallen into disfavor. Those who opposed the Dunses started using the name as a term of derision. The Dunses were dubbed ignorant and stupid, and by degrees any person who couldn't or wouldn't learn was called a Duns. In schools they were segregated and made to sit at dunstables. To show how established the practice was, there is a town not far from London called

Dunstable, where there must have been a large number of under-achievers. And to make matters worse, boys called Dunses and later dunces often had to sit on a stool in the corner and wear a tall conical cap of the sort worn by women. Dunces were sissies.

Thereby hangs the moral of the book that follows. Back of many words we know vaguely or half-know there are sometimes centuries of emotion. Words hide ideas and stories that must be explored. The words I have chosen are all tied up with religion, and each will tell you something about the background of our beliefs today. Like dunce, some of these words are by now far removed from their origin and even from their history.

Many religious terms have become a part of our common speech. Placebo, for example, is the name of any harmless sub-stance doctors give patients just to humor them. It has no drug. Placebo comes from the opening antiphon of the vespers for the dead in the Roman Catholic Church. It is the first person singu-lar of the Latin placere and means literally, "I shall please . . ."

Placebo is a good word for the opening of a book. There is nothing medicinal in the pages ahead of you. They aim simply to please and to prompt further discoveries of words related to religion.

Each word is a thing in itself. No fair reading more than one chapter at a time.

A IS FOR ADVENT

A is for Advent

A IS FOR ADVENT

Like the word adventure, advent is from the Latin ad and venire, meaning to come. Adventure tells us of something that is happening or is about to happen and advent tells us of the coming of an important event. The word has great dignity and is not to be used casually. Bergen Evans and Cornelia note that we speak of the arrival of a bus or plane but we speak of the advent of spring or of the age of steam.

Written with a capital A (the first letter in all alphabets), Advent is the first season of the church year. It commences on the Sunday nearest the day of St. Andrew the Apostle, November 30, and continues four weeks until Christmas. It announces a beginning and foretells the time when God will be revealed with special vividness. The idea back of it is that man cannot comprehend an event so momentous as the coming of Christ without a sustained period in which he prepares his mind and heart.

Christmas does not begin with Christmas day, any more than the football season starts with the first game. There is bound to be a long period of training and practice. You hear it said that Christmas has become commercial and frantic. We may feel, as the mad shopper did in the cartoon, that Christmas is at our throats again. We think desperately of all the things we have to get ready. It is not Christmas, however, that suffers corruption. It is Advent. It leaves us frustrated because our energies are misspent. We prepare on only one level, the festive, and not on the level of the meditative.

The early church gradually saw the need of preparing the minds of people for the Feast of the Nativity. This Feast began to be celebrated in Rome before 350 A.D., but it was not until centuries later that the season of preparation was observed in various parts of Christendom. In those days Advent culminated not in Christmas but on January 6, the first day of Epiphany. Epiphany is from the Greek word for manifestation and it marked the visit of the Magi and the time when the Christ Child was revealed to the Gentiles. In the eleventh century Pope Gregory VII shortened the season and made it end at Christmas. The Protestant churches that arose after the Reformation accepted the Advent dates Gregory had set. Advent still ends at Epiphany in the Eastern Orthodox Church. But whatever date is chosen, Advent is a period of preparation leading to a moment of revelation.

Through the centuries customs have grown up in the West to remind us that every day in Advent has a meaning and should be used to prepare the mind progressively — to deepen our reflections and bring us nearer to Christmas as well as bring Christmas nearer to us. One is the Advent calendar. Whether home-made or store-bought, the calendar has twenty-eight tiny decorated doors or windows, numbered for every day of the season.

Opened, each door reveals a scene or verse of Scripture chosen to carry forward the imagination.

As with any device, the value of the calendar depends on the way it is used. The same goes for the Advent wreath, which grew out of a decorated pagan cartwheel once used in Germany. Adapted to Advent, the wreath, laid flat, has a place for four large candles in appropriate colors to mark the weeks; or it may have twenty-eight small candles to mark the days. Lighting the candles as the season unfolds is attended by some simple religious ceremony the family works out.

That Advent customs have been carried on through generations shows how many realize the need of aids to keep our minds on something besides cooking and shopping as Christmas approaches. The singing of carols can be such an aid if not confined to impromptu wandering on Christmas eve. There needs to be rehearsal, memorizing, a study of the parts, attention paid to the meaning of the words. The very act of preparing to sing carols may cultivate the inner life and bring about the practice of harmony and goodwill.

Thoughtful reading can be a preparation for Advent. There are many stories suited to the season. One of my favorites is Henry van Dyke's *The Other Wise Man*. The name of the hero was Artaban. He started off with high hopes and precious jewels to join the Magi. But he missed the rendezvous because he delayed to help a wayfaring man who was ill. Artaban never found the Christ Child; at every turn he found and ministered from his means to someone in need. His reward at the end was to hear a voice saying, "Inasmuch as ye have done it unto the least of these, ye have done it unto me."

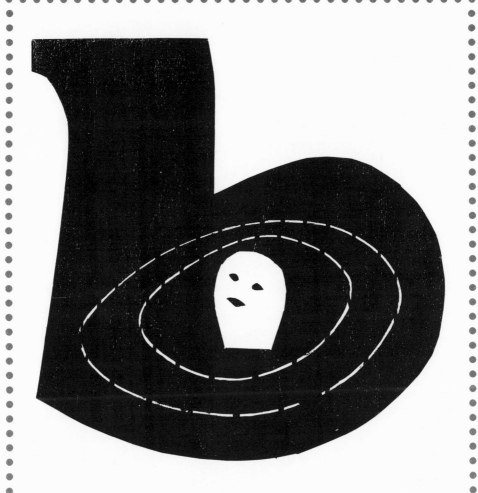

B is for Baptism

B IS FOR BAPTISM

So many picturesque uses have been made of the word baptism that some people ask if it is a religious word. Many of these uses have to do with war. It is common to read that a soldier going into battle for the first time gets his baptism of fire. This saying belonged to a period when war was thought to be romantic and good for men. But even in a new dictionary a newspaper is quoted as speaking of the official baptism of a new battleship.

These uses are odd, but they show the visual emotion assosociated with the word. Baptism is the first sacrament of the Christian ritual, without which other sacraments cannot be administered. It is in all branches of Christianity the initiation into the faith. It is the symbolic act of cleansing. The words for bathe and baptize come from the same Greek root.

This root, baptizein, is also the root of a great deal of organized difference of opinion about the method that ought to be used. Baptizein describes the act of plunging into, dipping, immersing. Certain churches build their faith around immersion as

[7]

the only proper form of baptism. Some reason from architecture to show that immersion was the original method of Christian baptism. Buildings where baptism took place were called baptistries — from the Greek word for bathing places. Some were round and some were hexagonal and at the center was a sunken pool surrounded by columns. Baptistries gradually disappeared, replaced by baptismal fonts near the altars of churches.

Religious groups who believe that baptism should be by sprinkling or pouring water only on the head argue the case of early baptism from art rather than architecture. And they point out the variety of ways in which the word baptize is used in the New Testament. It does not always suggest immersion. In some cases it describes a simple act of washing, in others an outpouring from above. It does always suggest cleansing. My father, who was a Methodist preacher, had a sermon in which he pointed out that sprinkling could be used in all or most circumstances where a person might want to be baptized. It was practical, applicable everywhere.

Churches that advocate sprinkling do not always insist upon this method. Churches that believe in immersion require it. These churches stem from the views and practices of a group of reformers in the sixteenth century. These reformers the orthodox scornfully called Anabaptists — from the Greek prefix ana, which meant again or anew. The Anabaptists insisted that, even if a person had been baptized as an infant, he must be baptized again to become a Christian, just as he must be born again. He must be immersed, dipped, thoroughly washed, cleansed for a new life. Plunging the whole body three times into the waters of

[8]

a stream or baptistry — in the name of the Father, the Son, and the Holy Ghost — became an established form and continues in our day among an immense body of Protestants.

In groups where immersion was not practiced and infant baptism continued, ceremonies related to baptism, but not a part of the sacrament, grew up. One was christening — or the giving of a Christian name to go along with the family name at the time of baptism. So widespread did the custom become that to christen came to mean to name. Ships and bells as well as babies were christened.

The other custom that arose out of infant baptism was that of having godparents stand sponsor for the child. It was the function of these to see that, in case the real parents failed to perform their Christian duties, the child continued upright and faithful. Baptism did not guarantee godliness or even goodness, but it was a dedicated start. Parents, flanked and backed by godparents, were to see that the christened child kept on the Christian path.

C is for Commandment

C IS FOR COMMANDMENT

Right after commandment in any dictionary comes commando. Commandment and commando have the same ancestry and yet the two words are so remote from each other in spirit that it is surprising to find them cheek by jowl. A commando was originally a member of a party called out, or commanded, for military purposes among the Boers — Dutch farmers in South Africa. The name bobbed up again in World War II to describe a special force in the British army. Commandos made heroic raids in enemy territory. The aim was to do as much damage as possible in the shortest possible time and then get away. Possibly.

A Commandment is one of the ten guiding laws given to Moses on Mt. Sinai. The word has a permanent and distinct meaning — you might say a technical one. Men don't go around giving commandments. Men give commands, if they are in a position to do so. Military usage and authority have made command a harsh and threatening word, but it stems from manus, the Latin word for hand and it means literally to place in the hands of. In this respect, command and commandment are related, for, according to the account of the delivery in Exodus, the Ten Commandments were placed in the hands of Moses. They were straight from God and it was the duty of Moses to pass them along to the people.

The scene was vested with high drama and circumstance. An exceedingly loud trumpet and much thundering and lightning summoned Moses to the top of the mountain, which smoked and quaked. The people were told to stand clear until the great transaction was done. God spoke the Commandments to Moses and then wrote them down on two stones. With these stones Moses returned to the people. But no sooner did he approach the place where the people were camped than he saw that they had made a golden calf and were dancing around it. Moses was so furious that he broke the stones on which the Commandments were graven and cast them to the ground.

Certainly the worship of the golden calf showed how much the Commandments were needed. The first was, *Thou shalt have no other gods before me*. Moses was summoned back later to Sinai and God wrote the Ten Commandments for him again. Then the stones were placed in the ark which Moses had built for them and there they remained until, according to tradition, the ark was hidden by Jeremiah at the time Jerusalem was taken by the Babylonians and has not been found again.

But they were remembered, partly because they were simple and not easily forgot. Some scholars think that they are best regarded as elementary rules for a half-civilized nation. All but one have a negative form, as befitted instructions for children.

One is positive: *Honor thy father and thy mother*. Honor in that day and time included feeding and clothing.

The Ten Commandments may be simple in form but they are profound in principle. They deal with situations that are likely to occur in any age. The Lord had said, "Thou shalt not make unto thee any graven image, or any likeness of anything that is in the heavens above, or that is in the earth beneath . . ." Yet with the Commandments in his hands Moses found the Children of Israel worshipping the golden calf, and in our day we continue to make graven images, not only of possessions and theories and status, but also of martyrs and heroes, substituting their likeness for God and putting them on pedestals.

There is a difference among religious bodies over the numbering of the Ten Commandments. The Catholics have one order or system, the Lutherans another, and other Protestant bodies a third. But however they are numbered, it is agreed that one group has to do with man's devotion to God and the other Commandments have to do with man's relation to his fellows. Jesus summed up the laws and made them positive and appealing to the heart when, asked to name the first commandment of all, he said, "Thou shalt love the Lord thy God with all thy heart, and with all thy soul, and with all thy mind, and with all thy strength; this is the first Commandment. And the second is like, namely this, Thou shalt love thy neighbor as thyself."

If you love the Lord with all your heart, soul, mind, and strength, you won't worship false gods and graven images. And if you learn to love your neighbor as yourself, you will not covet, lie, steal or cheat.

Ch is for Chapel

CH IS FOR CHAPEL

"Are you church or chapel?"

You will hear this question among British people who are trying to place each other by background. And in English novels you will find some characters referred to as chapel people. They belong to a nonconformist group, low in the social scale. They were not allowed to call the places they worshipped churches. Rather they were called chapels. Even in Shakespeare's day the difference in status between church and chapel was clear to the populace. In *The Merchant of Venice* the Bard of Avon has a character say, "If to do were as easy as to know what were good to do, chapels had been churches, and poor men's cottages princes' palaces."

The word chapel has many facets — little faces. In dictionaries you will see it defined as an association of printers and learn that once upon a time a printing house was called a chapel. In newspaper stories about strikes among printers you will occasionally find that a printers' union is referred as a chapel. This odd use of a word that seems altogether religious leads back to the story of the earliest days of printing in English. William Caxton was an English merchant who learned the printing trade at Cologne. He returned to England in 1476 and the place he set up his press was in the Chapel of Edward the Confessor. The Chapel was a part of Westminster Abbey and from here Caxton and his printers issued the first dated book in English. A group of men working in a chapel on anything so new and unusual as the printing of books came to be associated with their place of work. It was a pleasant and healthy association and by degrees the workers came to call their fellowship a chapel.

The word started out in Latin as a cappella, which means cloak or cape, and it was associated with a Roman soldier named Martin who was born about 316 A.D. Although a heathen and a soldier, Martin, according to the great tradition handed down to us, one day gave his cloak to a beggar he found shivering in rags. Not long after that Martin became a convert to Christianity and refused to fight. He lived as a hermit in a monastery near Tours, where he helped to train missionaries.

All through the latter years of his life Martin was much loved and his cloak was accepted as the symbol of heroic charity. The cloak became a relic, and a small house or chapel was built to keep it in, and the house itself came to be called after the cloak. It was a cappella. In French it was known as a chapelle and in English a chapel.

Not infrequently you hear of an a cappella choir, which is a choir that sings without accompaniment. A cappella means from the chapel, and the tradition of the chapel is plainsong. In the

Roman Catholic Church, although organs are widely used, they are still little more than tolerated and they have long been kept silent during parts of penitential seasons. Among some Protestant groups there is a strong objection to musical instruments of any kind in worship. Choral music without accompaniment is a cappella, whether it be in a chapel or a church.

There are chapels in homes, in churches, along waysides. A chapel continues to be a cloak, a quiet and personal place where the garment of devotion can be drawn around the shoulders, and the person who worships within feels for a moment alone and yet allied with the symbol of kindness and goodwill that goes back to the good legend of St. Martin.

D is for Disciple

D IS FOR DISCIPLE

If the word commandment has but one meaning, disciple has so many figurative uses that it is almost lost in the language. There is only one mention of disciple in the Old Testament and this is in connection with pupils in the music school of the temple. Disciple is used more than two hundred and fifty times in the New Testament and there is even reference to the disciples of the Pharisees. Matthew speaks of the seventy-two disciples of Jesus.

The word apostle appears only a few times in the accounts of the life of Jesus. It is applied to the twelve disciples he chose "that they might be with him and that he might send forth to preach." In Greek literature a herald empowered to arrange a truce was called an apostle. He undertook a mission with authority to act for the one who sent him.

A disciple, on the other hand, is an enthusiastic follower. Some lexicographers say that the word comes from the Latin verb discere: to learn; that it is allied to docere: to teach. From docere we get our English word docile to describe a person or thing that is teachable, or tractable. I have heard pilots and technicians refer to tremendous jet airliners as docile.

But one authority claims this line of derivation is a case of folk etymology and he sees a disciple as far from docile. He says that the word is formed from dis and the Latin verb capere, meaning to catch or take hold of, and that a disciple is one who seizes mentally, catches the infectious enthusiasm of his leader. There is more of emotion involved than there is in the picture of a pupil sitting at the feet of a master. A disciple is one who has felt deeply the influence of his guru and wants to keep on learning.

Discipline is a word closely related to disciple in origin, although discipline has come to mean a rule of conduct imposed from above. It was and is greatly esteemed by the military mind, obedience being essential to war. In *The Prince,* a cold and analytical study of how to control men and society, Niccolò Machiavelli wrote: "A prince should therefore have no other aim or thought, nor take any other thing for his study, but war and its organization and discipline . . ."

For centuries, even in religious circles, many thought that discipline should be severe and unrelenting and that the more severe it was the better. Discipline was the name given a whip used as a part of penance to make a penitent realize how sinful he had been.

By degrees disciple and discipline are coming together again. Among professors a discipline means the field in which their interest lies. A professor may refer to being in the discipline of mathematics or of history or of science. In this case he becomes a disciple of that interest. The best and most reliable discipline is the discipline of interest because it creates a mood of learning and a disposition to grow. With interest as our guide, we are not merely pupils but students who want to know more. We become disciples in the sense that we are apprentices who would like to "seize, take hold of, apprehend."

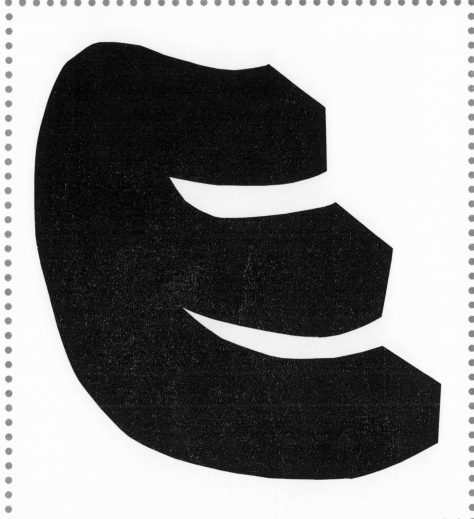

E is for Ecumenical

E IS FOR ECUMENICAL

Ecumenical is probably the newest old word in present speech. For it is old. You might say that **O** is for ecumenical because the early spelling, before it came into such wide use, was oecumenical. It meant worldwide or universal. And the old spelling helps toward understanding. The purpose of the ecumenical movement, as it is developing now, is to get everybody under one roof. The key to the big term is to be found in the Greek word for house: oikos. If religious people are not to come together under one roof, they are at least to feel at home in each others' houses.

There have been many ecumenical conferences, Protestant and Catholic. A conference that dealt with the worldwide affairs of a church body was called ecumenical to distinguish it from one that dealt with the affairs of only one area or region. But the term began to take on a much wider meaning when, in 1959, Pope John XXIII announced that he would assemble in Rome an ecumenical council to bring the worship and practices of the Roman

Catholic Church up to date. It was an audacious announcement, and John was such a liberal and hospitable person that many Protestants took his move to mean that he was going to hold open house for all faiths. John, once he detected this expectation, was quick to take advantage of the hopes raised. He set up a Secretariat for Christian Unity and invited observers from Protestantism and the Eastern Orthodox Church.

The Council convened October 11, 1962, in the huge basilica of St. Peter's with 2540 cardinals and bishops in attendance. It held four sessions before its work was concluded in October 1965. Pope John died in June of 1963 but the newly elected Pope Paul VI continued the Council. Meeting under full radio, television, and newspaper coverage, the sessions focused world attention on the efforts of church bodies to bring their faith and practice into harmony. Public interest and curiosity were immense. There seemed to be some prospect for a rapprochement between Protestant bodies and Rome and between Rome and the Eastern Orthodox Church. Protestant observers wrote about the Council and there was increasing talk about uniting denominations. From the Latin de and nomen, denomination simply means that a church is known by the name it is called.

Why shouldn't all the churches get together? To many the differences that divide religious groups seem absurd and some wonder why it takes so much ado to make them into a happy family. One who studies the differences, however, learns that they are of long standing and deep personal significance and that they cannot be quickly or casually resolved. There is a good deal of nostalgia in religion, and to a person brought up in one faith

[24]

such matters as the form of baptism or the form of church government are of high importance; and they will continue to be until the churches recognize the loftiness of their purpose and realize what they can do to set an example before the world. The example set by religious bodies has not been good. Since the slaughter and horrors of the Crusades, religion has been a divisive force in human affairs and has even set nations against each other.

Now the churches are beginning to think of the world and its welfare more than they think of their own identities. A spirit of concern has been growing quietly among many religious people for a long time. Ecumenism is news but it is not new. The headlines and the meetings merely bring it into the open, but if the interrelatedness of religious beliefs had not been present, there would be nothing to write or meet about.

Take the case of one religious leader who has caught the imagination of the world. Note how many diverse religious influences contributed to his views and feelings. The early ancestors of this man brought tribal beliefs out of Africa and his immediate ancestors were Baptist preachers. He went to a Baptist college but took his highest academic degree in a Methodist university. He then became a Baptist preacher in Georgia, which in colonial days had given hospice to persecuted Lutherans and Moravians. In seminary the Afro-American Baptist was deeply touched by the words of a preacher just back from India, where he had learned of the work and teaching of a Hindu, Mohandas K. Gandhi. The Georgia Baptist adopted the methods of the Hindu as methods fitting and proper to gain the rights of his

[25]

fellows and he applied principles similar to the Quakers' in his quest for justice and fair play. So widely recognized as religious was his work that Pope Paul gave it his blessing. And the man, together with his father before him, bore as his Christian name the name of the person whose beliefs led to the founding of one of the largest Protestant denominations and is credited with bringing about the Reformation: Martin Luther.

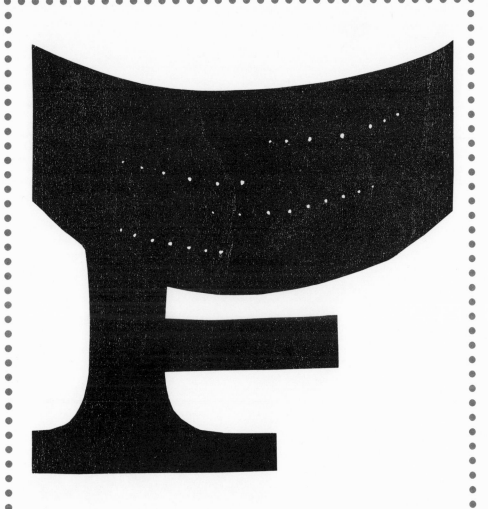

F is for Firmament

F IS FOR FIRMAMENT

Certain words have an inherent beauty. This beauty is part of their meaning. Firmament is such a word. It calls the mind from idle wanderings into a sudden awareness of mysteries that are beyond quick comprehension. Perhaps it does this because the word is unforgettably fixed and made luminous by the Psalmist: "The heavens declare the glory of God; and the firmament showeth his handiwork." Early Hebrew writers peopled the world and what lies around it and beyond it with forms that are akin to us, so that Job is reminded of the time when, before man, "the morning stars sang together."

If you take a detached and scientific view of the universe, the firmament vanishes before your eyes like a mirage. The firmament is not permanent, save as a magnificent idea, an early reminder of God's greatness. In the Psalmist's day it was a shield or canopy over the earth, firm enough to support the heavens above, where God dwelt. It was, in Job's words, as strong as a molten mirror. In one beguiling passage he saw the movement of the winds across the sky as God's breathing on the surface in order to polish it.

According to its Hebrew root, the word firmament was something beaten out as fine as one might beat out gold leaf. There were windows in the firmament and through these God released rain or snow or hail at his pleasure. God dwelt above the firmament but he could communicate with earth through it and he could come down to earth through it, as men often petitioned him to do: "Oh that thou wouldst rend the heavens, that thou wouldst come down, that the mountains might flow at thy presence."

With all its vastness and grandeur, the firmament was only a detail, only a part of Creation. It was but a part of God's handiwork. In early meanings, the word is tied up with bench or seat or footstool. In a sense, the firmament was God's footstool. One passage in Isaiah speaks of God sitting upon the circle of the earth, "and the inhabitants thereof are as grasshoppers."

Times change and so do words and ideas have to expand to keep up with the change. Today the areas outside the environs of our minor planet we call space, a word that means distances extending in all directions without limit. The very idea is as exciting as the firmament was to the Psalmist. Enormous telescopes have increased our vision and given us a first-hand picture of what lay beyond the ken of the Psalmist. New constellations and galaxies swim before us. Everywhere we turn we find order, and the word heavens has given way to the word cosmos — from Greek and Latin words meaning order. Order is everywhere. If we look through a microscope, we see a microcosm, a tiny universe in order. If we look through a telescope, we see a macrocosm, a big universe functioning the way we suppose it is supposed to. Of course there may be random departures in the system, just to keep us wondering. But in the main there is order.

It all makes the firmament seem out-of-date, but it is still there, and it shows more handiwork than devout writers, with all their inspired imagination, ever suspected.

G is for Genesis

G IS FOR GENESIS

In ancient times it was the custom to call a book by the word with which it began. If a book had begun "Once upon a time," the title would have been *Once*. The opening word in the Hebrew original of the first book of the Bible was bereshith, and it meant, In the beginning. When this book was translated from Hebrew into Greek, the Greek word for bereshith was genesis — and Genesis became the title. It is a book of beginnings, straight, simple, and steadfast in its narrative style, not pausing for argument. It says, in substance, "This is the way it was."

The fact that Genesis and the other books of the Old Testament were translated into Greek some two hundred years before the time of Christ tells us a lot about the world of that time and the popularity of the Genesis story. Greek was the language widely used. It was not the highbrow Greek of the classics but the plain talk language of ordinary people — the koine glossa, this being the Greek phrase for the common tongue.

We don't know exactly what date the Old Testament was

put into Greek, but we may assume that it was a rush job because the result was called the Septuagint. This was the Greek word for seventy, and tradition has it that the whole job was done in seventy days by seventy-two scholars.

The story goes that Ptolemy II, called Ptolemy Philadelphus, an enlightened monarch who made Alexandria a center of culture and had a lively interest in books, summoned Hebrew scholars who knew Greek to Egypt and put them under his high priest, giving them a deadline at the end of seventy days to make the translation for his royal library.

Whatever truth there is in the legend, at least the Old Testament was put into Greek. Jewish traders had their sacred books in the language they used from day to day, and the Hebrew heritage could now be read and spread among those who were not Jews. The Septuagint established itself in the literature of the day. Jesus was familiar with it. While he spoke Aramaic, a Semitic language, some of the statements of his that are recorded in the New Testament are direct quotations from the Septuagint translation.

Of all the books of the Old Testament, Genesis got and continues to get the most attention by far. More books have been written about it than all the other books of the Bible. There have been scores of accounts of creation and the beginning of man, but none has caught the fancy and held it with such constant appeal as the matter-of-fact, no-nonsense story of Adam and Eve and Abraham, Isaac, and Jacob. It is so convincing that millions have believed it to be literally true in all of its details. And those who don't believe it pay it the compliment of discussing it endlessly and using the names of its main characters and its stern morals to prove points.

Where is the person, old or young, who has not heard of the coat of many colors, of the man who sold his birthright for a mess of pottage? Who does not know of Cain as the world's first murderer, who refused to be his brother's keeper? Of Noah and the Ark and the rain that fell for forty days and nights? These characters and events have worked their way into the folk wisdom of the race and into titles such as *The Woman Thou Gavest Me* and *Ol' Man Adam an' His Chillun.* They belong to us all.

Nor are we unaware of the ideas in Genesis. Few who can read and write could fail to tell you the source of the words, "In the beginning God . . ."

Gn is for Gnostic

GN IS FOR GNOSTIC

Gnosis, the Greek word for knowing, is likely to turn up in many places, some of them remote and unexpected. This is because the Greeks set so much store by knowledge. You'll find the word in gnostic, of course, in diagnostic and prognosis, and you'll also find it in agnostic, the man who, as Webster puts it, doubts knowability.

That men could be classified on the basis of being knowers and non-knowers shows how important some people think certain knowledge is. It's a way of dividing the sheep from the goats, the men from the boys, and brings to mind Robert Benchley's line that the world is divided into two kinds of people, those who believe that there are two kinds of people and those who don't.

In the early days of the Christian church there arose a group of sects that carried over from the Greeks certain ideas about religion. These ideas had to do with enlightened learning. The members of the sects were known quite properly as Gnostics and they had wide influence for about three hundred years. They

[37]

believed that only those who achieved wisdom based on profound knowledge would be set apart for eternal life. The Gnostics were men of mind and they taught that only a few aristocrats of the mind made up the elect. Common folk would have to suffer forever in outer darkness. And that though the possession of gnosis "saved the initiates from the clutch of matter," some men need not apply. They were written off as corporeal and called hylic (made of wood: blockheads).

Such views, along with the claim that Christ was only a divine attribute personified, made the Gnostics the first body of heretics in the young Church. Heresy comes from the Greek word for choice, and the Gnostics posed a question that was to disturb the Christian world for hundreds of years to come: How much choice in belief could a person have and still be counted a Christian?

The Gnostics were absorbed by another cult, but strange ideas kept turning up in various hues and guises until the Church had to deal with the problem of official belief. The machinery set up in 1231 to combat heresy was the Inquisition. Pope Gregory IX sent into France inquisitors to act in his name against those found to have departed from the faith. The Inquisition spread to most of Europe, but not to Scandinavia, and it was rarely used in Germany or in England.

The extreme penalty for heresy was death by burning at the stake, and if only one heretic had been burned, the horror of it should have been enough to make Christendom shudder. But the procedures of the Inquisition, orderly at first, were subject to much abuse, and it brought about frightful injustices as well as inhuman cruelties. In Spain it fell under the control of the state and was used as a device to rid the population of elements considered undesirable by King Ferdinand and Queen Isabella and their Grand Inquisitor Thomás de Torquemada. At least two thousand heretics were burned in Spain during a short period, most of them Jews or Moors — converted Christians who were charged with having lapsed into their original belief.

A later Spanish king, Philip II, revived the Inquisition with the hope of ridding his country of Protestants. As late as 1559 he witnessed the burning of twelve heretics. The ceremony was called an auto-da-fé: an act of faith.

In time heresy trials proved futile. There were too many heretics to punish; and they began to organize churches of their own. Cruelty toward persons who differed in belief went on in religious wars, but penalties for individual heresy, never as severe elsewhere as they were in Spain, got milder. When Galileo, Italian astronomer and physicist, supported the Copernican theory, he was summoned to Rome and found guilty of heresy. But he was not burned — simply forced to recant. The story goes that when he finished his denial that the earth was, as he had said, a body that moved around the sun, he rose from his knees and whispered, "Nevertheless, it moves."

There was a new mood. Men were free to think as they chose. Bold ones outside religious organizations were called freethinkers and, much later, agnostics. They made a cult of not knowing. There is no reference to God in its derivation, but when a man calls himself an agnostic it usually means that he does not believe positively in God — is not even sure of God's existence.

In time even atheists were tolerated, if not considered respectable. The atheist differs from the agnostic in that he is much more emphatic. Theo is the Greek word for God, and the prefix in a-theoist means without. The atheist gets along without God. And frequently he believes that everyone should; that the physical world can be explained in physical terms and doesn't need a First Cause.

Both the atheist and the agnostic have a trait in common. They think about Theo or the absence of Theo a great deal. They are not indifferent, and take the trouble to deny his existence and discuss his improbability. They are very inclined to worry themselves and others about what lies back of the universe. The agnostic doesn't know, the atheist denies, but they often give more attention to the subject of God than the person who claims to be a true believer. Isn't that ironic?

H is for Halloween

H IS FOR HALLOWEEN

Among the rough and rowdy Celts, who once occupied part of what now is England, New Year's Eve fell on October 31, and it was the wildest night of the year. The Celts (or Kelts if you prefer) had poured across from Europe a thousand years before the time of Christ. They were a fierce and barbaric people and their religion was not unlike their temper. The priests of the Celts were Druids. One of the festivals the Druids presided over was the Eve of Samhain, marking the end of summer and the beginning of winter. At this festival on October 31 the Druids sought to placate Samhain, the Lord of Death. Some say that Samhain on this night called back the souls of the wicked who had died the previous year; others say that Samhain permitted the souls of all the departed to spend a few hours in their former homes, even to warm themselves at the old family fireside. In either case, it was the night the dead came back. The inhabitants of the spirit world were turned loose, including witches, who liked to get together on the Eve of Samhain for one of their conventions and they came riding broomsticks, accompanied by their black cats.

For all their warring savagery, the Celts were well organized. They lived in tribes and villages. Their society was marked by layers of status and it was governed by priests and chiefs and nobles. They were an industrious people and they had brought with them from Europe their skill in ironmongery. They knew how to fashion both wheels and weapons, and it was under the Celts that the strong plow and the ancient Greek chariot took their places on English soil. Perhaps such a well-ordered people needed a night to howl. Certainly they found it on the Eve of Samhain. Anybody could do anything he wanted to and blame the pranks and the results on demons let loose for the night. The mischief was officially approved.

Then, early in the first century Anno Domini, the Year of Our Lord, the conquering Romans appeared and took over. But not immediately and not completely. In due course they set up their own Julian calendar which meant that the new year began in January instead of November. Yet October 31 continued to be celebrated as All Witches Night. Old customs do not die peacefully, especially if they provide a chance to raise the devil.

Not until the Roman legions left in A.D. 597 did Christianity come to England. It came chiefly in the person of a Roman monk named Augustine. This particular Augustine was a missionary and he brought forty monks with him to help civilize the English. The whole band was received kindly by King Ethelbert of Kent, who embraced the Christian faith and gave the monks an old Roman church in his capital — Canterbury.

[44]

Now began a slow permeation of English life by the Church. It set out to bring practices into line with its own ideas of reverence. One custom it changed was All Witches Night. Two hundred years after the coming of Augustine, Pope Gregory III declared November 1 as an English holiday for all saints, known and unknown. The Anglo-Saxon word for holy was halga. A saint was a holy man, hence a hallow. The day appointed would be All Hallows Day and the night before it became All Hallows Eve.

Of course the Church could not change conduct by changing the name of a holiday. In old England and ultimately new America, over the centuries, strenuous pranks continued to be the order of the evening. Gates were hoisted from their hinges and hidden. Wheels were taken off buggies and wagons. Clotheslines were strung acros walks and paths. The night remained Celtic. Whatever was done could be blamed on the license of the occasion. Or so the theory ran.

By degrees, however, symbols and images became more prominent than pranks. Children went about in mad costumes and demanded treats or sweets or coins as a tribute for the protection of property. They were generally placated. Then, one Halloween in 1950, Sunday school pupils in a small community started collecting coins, not for themselves, but for the welfare of the world's less fortunate children. They raised thirty-six dollars and sent it to the United Nations International Emergency Children's Fund. The amount raised was only a mite but it marked a step toward hallowing Halloween. The example started a new pastime. Now the children of thirteen thousand communities collect more than two million dollars each year. It is money, *The Christian Century* says, "to exorcise the demons of hunger, poverty, disease, ignorance and fear that torment eight hundred and fifty million of the world's billion children."

more

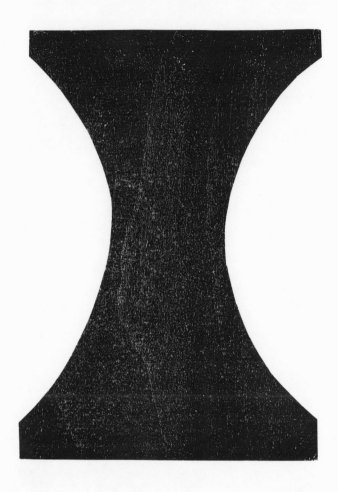

I is for Immortality

I IS FOR IMMORTALITY

"Every exit here is an entrance somewhere else." This line from a Broadway play, *Rosencrantz and Guildenstern Are Dead,* suggests to any sensitive or speculative mind that life goes on. And on. It strikes me as a pithy summary of a great deal of man's thinking about immortality — the belief that, while we are obviously mortal, we do not really die but live forever.

How and where we live is another matter, and on this point there are many thoughts in many religions. One comes out of Hinduism, a religion of the East with multiplied millions of adherents: transmigration. The soul migrates across the barrier of death and lives again in another body or form, possibly that of an animal. Another name for this belief is metempsychosis, from Greek words meaning change of soul. What your soul passes into at the time of change depends on the kind of life you have led in the body you have just left. If you have been petty and nasty, you might come alive again as a louse and have to work your way back up again. Sobering thought.

A refined form of belief in the reappearance of the soul is called reincarnation. The root here is the Latin word for flesh: carne. Reincarnation means taking on flesh again. If you are reincarnated, you come back in the body of another person. It is not clear where you are meanwhile or how the next body is chosen, but reincarnation teaches that the self-conscious self can be kept intact and improved upon each return. To inherit eternal life one must be born again and again. There is no slipping back into animal bodies. Reincarnation assumes progress from one embodiment to the next, an endless cycle of opportunities that lead to ultimate perfection. It teaches that the conscious self exists before birth and will continue to exist after death.

In the West, and especially in America, we have an acute sense of personal identity and modern interpretations of reincarnation appeal to us. The individual wants to survive as a personality. Being an activist surrounded by, or with the prospect of attaining, success and comfort, he does not want immortality in general but his own. This is for him the crux of the matter. A publication of the Theosophical Society in America assures us: "All the qualities we now possess, of body, mind and soul, are the result of our use of our ancient opportunities, and the use we make of our present opportunities will determine our future character and capacity."

The sense of personal identity is by no means universal in thoughts about immortality. Men who reflect deeply may be happy to think of themselves as part of the life force. And the experience among some primitive peoples shows us that the ego is not always tied up with survival. Margaret Mead gives us a moving account of rites among the Balinese. There is no weeping at death, save for an infant. Then the mother is allowed to weep and relatives digging the grave reproach the child, saying, "The next time you come, stay longer and at least eat rice with us before you go." After cremation the bones are laid out in the form of a skeleton. Little girls take the soul from the body and carry it in their arms like a baby to the household temple for rest and refreshment and then return it. In the whole disposal of the body, which ends when the bones are pounded into ashes and set out to sea in tiny canoes, the sense of identity, as Margaret Mead observes, is only ceremonial.

Forms differ but concern remains. The dead are not ignored, and any kind of respect for the dead, as in ancestor worship, is a part of the total feeling about immortality. Ancestor worship was usual among the Greeks and Romans and in China and Japan. The departed had status and were often thought to dwell among the gods. The Egyptians, aided by the climate, did the most remarkable job of preserving the bodies of the dead, just in case the soul wanted to return and take up abode again. Some Egyptian mummies are five thousand years old, swathed in linen bandages treated with gum or resin, and still outwardly in good condition.

Then there are those who believe that we can achieve immortality, that we live on in our children or in the influence we cast on others or in the good works we do. Great artists attain immortality through what they create as perpetual reminders of their being. We speak of Beethoven in music, Titian in painting, Da Vinci in versatility as being among the immortals. On the tomb of Sir Christopher Wren in St. Paul's Cathedral, London, is the tribute to the man under whose guidance St. Paul's was built: "If you seek a monument, look about you."

But not all of us can be great artists and those who cannot must think in other terms. The Christian view of immortality is forthright and distinct. It is that Jesus was crucified and buried in a tomb with a heavy stone rolled against the entrance and that he arose from the dead and appeared to his disciples in the flesh. Only one disciple, Thomas, doubted when he heard the news and he was convinced later when he talked with Jesus. The resurrection was a fact to early Christians and it was more than a fact because Jesus was accepted as more than a man. He was Man and God in one, and if he arose as Man, all who believed would also live again.

J is for Jude

J IS FOR JUDE

For a long while I thought that Thomas Hardy's novel *Jude the Obscure* might be about St. Jude, who was about as obscure as a man can get and be known at all. Today he is spoken of as The Forgotten Saint. Actually, Hardy's novel is a grisly story of English country life in the nineteenth century, but at least we know that the name Jude was well enough remembered and thought of that Hardy gave it to his main character.

Jude was one of the Twelve Apostles who shared the Last Supper with Jesus and he is hardly less known than the others in this chosen group. Ask the next person you meet to name the Twelve and he is likely to start off bravely with Matthew, Mark, Luke and John, and then fall silent while he tries to bring others out of his memory. He has given you the names of the men who wrote the first four books of the New Testament. Only Matthew is considered by scholars probably to have been an Apostle; John may possibly have been. Mark and Luke were not. Matthias was chosen by the eleven to replace Judas Iscariot.

The name Jude is a variant of Judas. It appears only once in the Bible and then as the name of the author of the shortest book — twenty-two verses. The writers who tell the story of Jesus and his companions are at pains to see that there is no chance to confuse Jude with the betrayer of Jesus. John goes so far as to refer to him as "Judas, not Iscariot." And on the list of the Twelve given in the tenth chapter of Matthew he appears as "Labbaeus, whose surname was Thaddeus."

But there is no doubt that, although his identification tag was vague, Jude was one of the Twelve. And the Twelve were distinguished for all time, Jude among them, for their daring. They went out to preach a startling new idea to a world that was indifferent, then suspicious, then hostile and murderous. The word martyr comes from the Greek word for witness. In the days of the Apostles a witness was one who testified and he knew that he was likely to be done to death for his witness. All of the Twelve who went forth on preaching missions were martyred, save one, but not until they had carried the idea of love taught by Jesus far and wide and established in men's minds the knowledge that members of the new sect would die rather than kill.

Tradition has it that Jude went to Persia, where he engaged in a contest with two magicians and proved their prophecies wrong. Next he made a prophecy of his own, which proved right. But, although he was popular for a time, the demands of the new belief he proclaimed made enemies among those who did not want to abandon their old way of life and Jude was killed, some say by arrows, some say by clubs.

Jude was a saint by consent long before any ecclesiastical

machinery had been set up to declare men and women officially holy. After his death believers began to pray in his name, asking him to intercede with God in their behalf, and over the centuries so many were so successful in their petitions through him that Jude became known as the saint of the impossible.

You could say also that this Apostle is the saint of the saintless. Jude is dear to many who, while not practicing Christians, like to think that there is a holy man appointed by tradition and practice to befriend sinners and wayfaring men. The name of St. Jude appears in personal columns of newspapers and is always associated with those who are in desperate straits.

For all his record and reputation, the saint of the impossible remains a shadowy figure and in our day there is more publicity than information about him. Once when Danny Thomas was only a struggling night club singer and wondering if he had a future, a friend told him of a remarkable cure that had come to pass after a prayer to St. Jude. Danny, a devout Catholic, said, "Who's St. Jude?" He found out fast. Later, in gratitude for help he felt he had got through St. Jude, Danny raised millions of dollars to build a children's hospital and named it for The Forgotten Saint.

How many good people there are we may never hear of! Study the courage and zeal of Jude and the other Apostles and you realize how much we are in debt to the obscure, to persons who worked for human good without worldly reward. We are, as St. Paul wrote in his Letter to the Hebrews, compassed about with a great cloud of witnesses. And witnesses today are not martyrs.

K is for Kerygma

K IS FOR KERYGMA

Most of us have had the experience of hearing or seeing a word for what we are sure is the first time and then, mystery of mysteries, hearing it or seeing it again the same day or soon thereafter. It happened to me with scrimshaw. At a party one night I was the only one present who had not heard the word and did not know that scrimshaw is the name for carving on ivory or shell. Next morning I got up early to read the manuscript of a book on vocabulary. And what was the second word on the third page? You guessed it.

Kerygma has been in and out of use for centuries. Today it is coming back into vogue, as words have a way of doing, although I found it in only two of the five dictionaries I consulted when I first began to hear about it. I found it also in *A Theological Word Book of the Bible,* but there, just to mix me up, it was spelled kerugma. It is from a Greek word, keryssein, meaning to proclaim. As used by theologians and students of early Christianity it describes the act of heralding the Kingdom of God, of

[59]

proclaiming that Christ was God and that in the death and resurrection of Christ men might have eternal life.

Through kerygma, as through a magnifying glass, we can get some sense of the scenes at the time that the news of the Christ first smote men's minds. The news came suddenly, with no preparation or warning, and it brought a blast of ideas that had not been seriously considered before. There were other religions, but they were fixed. Judaism had had its early dramas of thunder and fire and revelation, but it was established and quiet and respectable when the Apostles went out. Here were twelve common Jews saying that a Jew called Jesus of Nazareth was in fact the Son of God and that he had been crucified dead and buried and that he had risen from the dead and ascended into heaven. What's more, all this had happened but a short while before. It was not something handed down by tradition but a living event and it was to usher in a changed world.

This was the astonishing message carried by the Apostles. There is nothing in our experience to compare it with, although we can get some impression from the commotion stirred by dedicated members of the hippie sect. The Apostles offered a new body of belief that made men willing to die, but not to kill, for an inward light. And it was not merely the belief that dumbfounded the Graeco-Roman world. It was the audacity of proclaiming it. This was what men later, looking back on the sight, were to call kerygma.

What interests students of religion in our time and helps bring back the word kerygma is their feeling that the essence of the Christian idea has been lost in folderol (folderol was originally a meaningless refrain used in old songs). Early Christians had the excitement of discovery, the elation of finding a truth for the first time. The word preach comes from the Latin praedicare and it also means to proclaim. The preachers in Apostolic Days proclaimed Christ to those who had not heard of him before, and later preachers heralded the story to those who heard it rarely. But after two thousand years of fragmentary repetition the news gets distorted by familiarity.

Is there any way, earnest thinkers ask, that we can recover the zeal of the Apostles? There was a tremendous power in and around kerygma. To find the sources of it may be the best way of introducing it again. A great period of proclamation that so vitally affected humankind deserves close study. You can reason from effect to cause.

Imagine what the world would have been like without kerygma — if the teachings of Jesus had been left quietly in literature as nothing more than a body of ethical concepts. Then imagine what our world would be like if we suddenly rediscovered those teachings and saw what they implied and how they could be applied. There is a remarkable book called *In His Steps* by Charles M. Sheldon. The fact that it has sold twenty million copies in all lands and languages gives you an idea of its appeal. It's the story of a preacher who is led to decide that he will try to act in every situation he confronts exactly as he thinks Jesus would act. Members of his congregation join him in the covenant. Needless to say, there is no lack of plot or complications. The story is laid in the late nineteenth century. If it were laid in our day it would have even more complications.

In His Steps helps to show that we might recapture the rapture of the first Christians if we but understood Christianity as a religion of love and if we sought to work it into every nook and cranny of our political and social life.

That might bring about a new kerygma.

more

L is for Love

L IS FOR LOVE

One trouble with love is that there is only one word for it. There are many terms of endearment but they are not the same and they are not verbs; they do not express feeling in action. We don't say, "I affection you." We may say, "I cherish you." But that's an elaboration, a second statement of the idea. There is no synonym for love, and we use the word in a score of ways, ranging from "I love artichokes" and "Love-All" to tell of a tie in a tennis game to the simple expression, "I love you."

Sometimes the origin and history of a word help us to use it better. But in the case of love there is not much help from history. Out of German, Anglo-Saxon, and other languages you get only nuances or shades of meaning. In Middle High German it meant to show kindness and in the Latin lubere it meant to please. As in other tongues, so it is in English. The differences in our use of the word are so delicate that we must often convey our sentiment by tone and gesture, by lilt or solemnity.

The Hebrews had the same problem because they had only

one word to cover many acts and emotions. But they made the word work. It described physical desire and also kinship and friendship. Then they took the word and extended it to picture the relation between the mass of people and Jehovah. The idea that a people and a god could love was unique. It stood in stark contrast to the beliefs and practices of other religions. Greek philosophy, for example, held that the gods were as much above people as people were above inanimate objects and, as one writer put it, "It would be preposterous if anyone said he *loves* Zeus!"

Yet the Hebrews said that not only did the people love Jehovah, exalted and high above the earth though he was, but also that Jehovah loved his people. The belief had the essential element of love, namely, that it went both ways. It was reciprocal. Jehovah loved persons as well as the people in general. He walked with Adam in the cool of the evening and he called Israel "the seed of Abraham, my friend." What makes the Hebrew stories so convincing is that the Lord loved without approving the things his people did. The prophets reproached the people for their vile conduct and neglect. Yet God was willing to forgive and he was often kindly affectioned toward his people. The proponents of the idea of God love seemed to understand, as a friend of mine remarked, that we need love most when we deserve it least.

The idea of fellowship between God and man would astound us if we suddenly stumbled on it for the first time. It has been built into our beliefs so much that we have lost sensitiveness to its meaning. Today, with science constantly exploring the mysteries of the microcosm and the macrocosm, it may sound ridiculous. It supposes that God is like us, subject to the emotions we read into Him. But there it is, a stark fact of history, buttressed by centuries of writings and continued belief. It provides the background and setting of the teachings of Jesus, which tell us to love even our enemies. The ideal of love continued to grow among those who caught the spirit and implications of Jesus and reached its peak in John's statement, "God is love."

In a word, the association of God and love is present from the beginning in Judaism and it is made the quintessence of the Christian faith. It is present also in our modern thinking, whether we acknowledge it or not. Joyce Cary, the distinguished British novelist who wrote perceptively of art and people, once said to me, "If you believe in altruism, you believe in God." I did a double take on his remark. I nodded casually at the time. It was months before the real meaning of Cary's words overtook me. What he said was an up-to-date philosophical way of stating the old tie between our love of our fellows and our love of God. The two have been joined for ages and the importance of the union is clearer all the time.

Love is a word of many brilliant facets, but there is nothing more remarkable about it than the fact that men have dared think that love permeates the cosmos.

M is for Miracle

M IS FOR MIRACLE

M might be for manna because manna was a miracle. It fell as the gentle dew from heaven in the passing of the night and formed into a bread that tasted like wafers and honey. And it came at a time when the Children of Israel murmured against their leaders, Moses and Aaron, who had led them up out of the land of Egypt into a wilderness near Sinai, where there was naught to eat; and the Children of Israel longed for the fleshpots of Egypt and feared lest all die of hunger.

Then manna came. And the people marveled. Quail came, too, and the people had meat to eat. But quail they had seen before; the manna was strange and new and sudden. They didn't even know what to call it, and the origin of the word is obscure. In some dictionaries manna is still defined by a question: *What is it?*

This was the question the Children of Israel asked when they beheld manna. And it was the question the people in Jerusalem asked when a crowd watched Jesus raise his friend Lazarus from the grave after he had been dead four days. As the stone covering the entrance of the cave where Lazarus had been laid was rolled away, Jesus called in a loud voice, "Lazarus, come out!" And, as *Today's English Version of The New Testament* tells it, "The dead man came out, his hands and feet wrapped in grave cloths, and a cloth around his face. 'Untie him,' Jesus told them, 'and let him go.' "

Our English word miracle is a descendant of the Latin words mirari, meaning to wonder, and mirus, meaning wonderful. Other words in common use come from the same roots, including mirror, which causes people to wonder and admire; and admire itself is from the same source. So is mirage, a great body of water reflected on the desert or in dry places.

A kind of miracle in itself is the fact that, as the word for miracle evolved through various languages, it got itself tied up with the word smile. In Old English and Middle English and Scandinavian languages miracle and smile go together. In some other languages the word miracle and the word laughter are related. A miracle pleases. It delights. It makes us smile or laugh for sheer joy that it came to pass.

A good deal of time has been spent by theologians in trying to explain miracles, to make them plausible — something to be applauded. Miracles seem to go against the laws of nature and many are inclined to reject them for this reason. Those who accept miracles, on the other hand, point out, as George Santayana does, that "miracles are propitious accidents, the natural causes of which are too complicated to be readily understood."

And it is true that we see all about us nowadays happenings

that would once have been considered contrary to the laws of nature. Gravity is a law of nature, and was before man defined it. Man could not go up in the air and move around there. A magic carpet was pure fancy, nothing you could actually ride. And a hundred years ago one who turned a knob and drew music out of the air would have been thought to be performing a miracle no less remarkable than manna. We may not believe in manna but we experience the miracle of music in the air.

In the magazine *New* Robert Tree West gives us this quick poetic picture:

Miracles? Miracles?
Let's not pretend,
They can all be explained
From beginning to end.
They're a trick, like the rabbit
That's pulled from a hat.
"I see," says Columbus,
"But radar, what's that?"

Wonders never cease! Scientists are now launched on a series of what they call planned discoveries. They are out to perform acts which no one believed possible, the latest being to make enough protein bacteria powder from a small amount of petroleum to feed the whole world. To millions among the hungry, their brains and bodies stunted now from a lack of protein, this new growth will be a miracle. But it's already been done in laboratories and men will keep working until it's done on a large scale.

Miracles show what is possible, not what is so. They beckon the imagination, and who is bright enough to know that they do not at times foreshadow what is to come?

N is for Neighbor

N IS FOR NEIGHBOR

One day a certain lawyer came up to Jesus and asked him what he must do to receive eternal life. Jesus asked him what the Scriptures said and how he interpreted them and the lawyer answered promptly, "Thou shalt love the Lord thy God with all thy heart, and with all thy soul, and with all thy strength, and with all thy mind; and thy neighbor as thyself." Jesus commended him for knowing and told him to act on what he knew. But the lawyer was not satisfied or perhaps he wanted an argument. He said, "And who is my neighbor?"

It was in answer to this question that Jesus told the Parable of the Good Samaritan, beginning, "A certain man went down from Jerusalem to Jericho, and fell among thieves . . ." The thieves stripped him and beat him and left him half dead. A priest came along soon after and saw the man's plight but passed by with no more than a glance. So did an official of the Temple. The person who stopped, tended the victim's wounds, took him to an inn and paid for his care and promised to come back later and pay more if it were needed, was a man of Samaria. And Samaria was a part of their country the Jews despised because it had a mixed population. Only the Samaritan had proved himself a neighbor because, as Jesus pointed out, he had shown mercy.

The story took the word neighbor beyond the practical and gave it a new and adjustable meaning, one that could be suited to the future and to any circumstance men might encounter. Our English word simply puts together two other words — nigh and boor. A neighbor was a farmer who lived near. For a long while the word had always to do with nearness. As early as 700 B.C. Hesiod, a Greek poet who wrote witty observations of daily life and work on the farm, noted that a bad neighbor is as great a misfortune as a good neighbor is a great blessing. It was plain even then that a man's life was intimately tied up with the behavior of others and that it behooved one to treat the fellow on the next farm well.

But as society got more complex the word neighbor needed a new and expanded definition. Sometimes words change to accommodate a new set of facts. The word kind grew out of the word kin. As people began to behave considerately to those beyond the family and the clan, a new word came into being. You were kind to more than kin. The word neighbor has kept its form, but the sense of it has increased and deepened. In 1586 it was used to mean being near to a person or place. By 1820 it was used in the sense of "being on neighborly terms with others."

The word had grown. It is still growing. When you can

turn a knob on a little black box in your living room and see another human being killed, really killed, in front of you, you know who your neighbor is. It's still the fellow next door, but it is also the man who lives in Vladivostok or works in a rice field. Every man on earth is my neighbor.

Thomas Mann has said that science has made us all neighbors and it is up to religion to make us brothers. Science and religion working and thinking together are needed to show that there are no foreigners any more. A new word that has lately come into the language gives us a glimpse of how vitally we are all related. The word is noösphere. It is not in the dictionaries yet but you occasionally see it in print and you hear it on the radio, pronounced nu-o-sfere. It was put into use by Pierre Teilhard de Chardin, French philosopher and scientist, who wrote a book called *The Phenomenon of Man*. Noösphere is made up of two Greek words: noo, for mind, and sphere, for ball.

Even to those of us who sit on the sidelines of science, the idea that the noösphere expresses offers great excitement. Teilhard saw the earth as made up of a series of circles or spheres. At the center is a circle of metals, topped by a circle or sphere of rocks. Around the surface of the earth is a sphere of water and of vegetation and trees. Above this is the atmosphere, the prefix atmos being Greek for vapor. Beyond is the noösphere, which is to be thought of as a globe-encircling membrane created by the mind of man, his reflections, aspirations, and accomplishments. There is something psychic as well as physical surrounding our world. The number of thoughts of decency and kindness and love of neighbor men send out are not only not in vain; they actually go to enhance the substance of the noösphere.

So N is for neighbor and, in the broadest sense, neighbor is for noösphere.

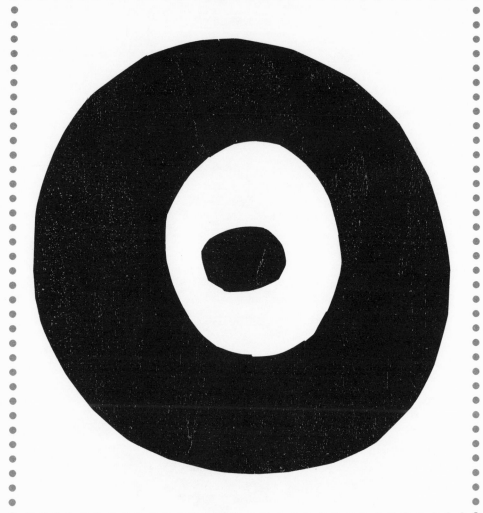

O is for Omnipotence

O IS FOR OMNIPOTENCE

We do something to words by the way we use them. And words take on the color and tone of the period in which they are used. Take the word power. It comes from the Latin potere, meaning to be able. Potent comes from another form of the same verb. Combine omni with potent and you get omnipotent or the quality of being all-powerful. But power is usually identified with might, with tremendous strength. Since ancient times we have thought of power as physical. Ovid, writing about the time of Christ, has this line, "Then the omnipotent Father with his thunder made Olympus tremble." When an omnipotent god was needed in the ancient Greek plays to alter the action and rescue characters beyond human help, an actor was brought to the stage by stage machinery. He was called a deus ex machina or a god from a machine. This phrase remains in our language and means any artificial device that suddenly appears and resolves difficulties.

With the advent of gunpowder and steam, our sense of a

physical God increased. God was thought of as having unlimited, infinite ability to intervene, to move things and people around. As the power of man increased, more ond more was expected of God.

Thinking of God as Superman is known as anthropomorphism — from the Greek words for man and form, meaning that we give God in our imaginings the stature of man and cling to bodily ideas about him. We have not yet learned to think of God in other ways. All-powerfulness is an idea we associate with God because it is the farthest stretch of our own conceit, something we cannot attain, with all our marvels.

Today men are thinking of God more as spirit than as force or naked power. They are seeing that there are other kinds of power besides those to which we have become accustomed since the beginning of modern warfare and the industrial age. As change comes about, our view of prayer changes from petition to communion and a sense of oneness with the universe. "Closer is he than breathing, nearer than hands and feet."

A friend of mine who pilots giant jets across the Atlantic was once asked if he ever prayed when he faced a crisis while responsible for a hundred or more people. "No," he replied, "I figure God didn't get me into this mess and He's not going to get me out of it." Thinking of God as omnipotent and a very present help in time of trouble encourages us to shift responsibility to him. The hymn that begins, "God the Omnipotent!" ends with the refrain, "Give us peace in our time, O Lord!" Peace is not likely to be given from on high. It will have to be brought about by human effort.

Of course the whole subject of omnipotence confronts us with some of the deepest perplexities of human experience. These are not likely to be resolved soon, though they are fascinating to discuss. Perhaps the safest plan will be to follow the old exhortation: "Work as if everything depended on you and pray as if everything depended on God."

P is for Prophet

P IS FOR PROPHET

The origin of the word prophet tells us that it has a triple meaning and is open to several interpretations. The Greek base of the word is phanai, meaning speak, but some sources say that the prefix pro means before and some say that it means for; and some say it means both. So a prophet may be said to speak for or to speak before. And if a prophet speaks before, what does he speak before? Before an event? Or before people?

Because of our incurable interest in the future, we usually think of a prophet as one who speaks before an event. He foretells. He gives us a vivid picture of the future — the more vivid the picture the better the prophet. Now and then he gives dates and details.

Probably the most famous of the foretellers was a French astrologer and physician named Michel de Nostredame, who wrote a book called *Centuries* and signed his name Nostradamus. The book was made up of rhymed prophecies and he made himself well known throughout Europe and in history. He predicted the manner of death of Henry II of France, who died of a wound received in a tournament. Many have read the prophecies of Nostradamus and looked backward and have figured that he foretold many events that came to pass the way he said they would.

Nostradamus was a man who worked with the stars. The prophet who foretells usually has some source of insight outside himself. He has a peculiar or special relationship with the divine or unseen forces. You realize this when you see the word divine used as a verb. A person may say that he is trying to divine what you mean. He wants to get what is hidden in your thoughts. Or a man may use a divining rod to find water or oil or minerals. Seers have long been said to practice the art of divination, seeking by unusual powers to get at what is not apparent on the surface.

The other kind of prophet speaks before people. He forthtells. You will find this type of prophet in the Old Testament — and hardly anywhere else. Amos, Hosea, Micah, Isaiah, and Jeremiah were among them. The prophets were no part of the formal religion of the Hebrews. They were voices crying in the wilderness. They spoke out against the oppression of the poor by the powerful. They called for justice and right conduct among rulers. They put behavior above piety and said that leading a good life was more important than following a ritual. Micah's words sum up much of their teaching: "He hath showed thee, O man, what is good: and what doth the Lord require of thee, but to do justly, and to love mercy, and to walk humbly with thy God?"

The prophets urged kings toward pacific measures instead

of wars and killing, toward compromise rather than conflict. Notable among the major prophets was Isaiah, who lived in the eighth century B.C. He was a man of noble eloquence, carrying a lyre and at times playing it to stress the rhythm of his speech, and it must have lent special force to what he had to say. Once when King Hezekiah was about to go to war with the Assyrians, Isaiah spoke against the action in these words: "For thus saith the Lord God, the Holy One of Israel; in returning and rest shall ye be saved; in quietness and confidence shall be your strength; and ye would not. But ye said, No; for we will flee on horses; therefore shall ye flee; and, We will ride upon the swift; therefore shall they that pursue you be swift." Choose weapons and weapons alone will decide the issue.

Jeremiah, who prophesied about a hundred years after Isaiah, addressed himself to the moral waywardness of the people. But he also warned against the futility of trying to resist Babylon, and for his pains was put in prison and in stocks. He was a sad man, given to lamentations and threats of doom. He was known as the weeping prophet, and to this day a tale of woe or an account that is full of lament and pity is known as a jeremiad.

It was not so much their sage political advice, however, that gave the prophets their singular and secure position in religion. Rather it was the fact that this advice sprang from lofty principles. These principles were not their own. They were Jehovah's. They did not pretend or claim to be God, but they spoke in his behalf to remind the people of his eternal standards. They knew, as one of the Proverbs embracing the folk wisdom of the

Hebrews phrased it, that where there is no vision the people perish. And the vision the prophets held up to men we still cannot dismiss. Writing in our day, Edith Hamilton says, "The prophets show us what we should be. The world they point us to cannot be given up as forever unattainable. The prophets' sense of values was sure. They knew unerringly what was important and what was not. Religion's work was to create a world where no one was oppressed."

To this end the prophets spoke fearlessly before kings and rulers, and they were forthtellers. Yet by the very dreams of the future they presented, they foretold. And in doing this they spoke for Jehovah — and for the highest hopes of man.

Ps is for Psalms

PS IS FOR PSALMS

Along with the speculation about which came first, the chicken or the egg, there is an equally fascinating one: Which came first, the harp or the psalm? The word psalm means a song sung to a harp, and it comes chiefly from the Greek word psallein, meaning to pluck or twang on a stringed instrument. The harp and the song are, as Mark Twain would put it, as inseparable as a pair of pants. One dictionary suggests that psalm is tied up with words meaning to grope or to touch softly. By this token you might think of the early Hebrew poets as sitting around and strumming harps, allowing the instrument to contribute to their thoughts as today's jazz musicians or folk singers might. One writer speaks of the harp strings of the mind and it may be that there are such things.

The earliest harps, which came out of Egypt, were simple. The discovery that strings would make music probably arose from a hunter or warrior in the act of twanging the string of his bow in idle or bored moments. Of course harps improved and got more complex, so that by the time of David they were quite musical. Many Psalms are attributed to David. It is likely that the improvement of the harp and of the Psalms went together.

Not a few of the Psalms seem personal and it may be that these were composed and sung by lonely men or men alone. But after the Jews returned to Palestine in 538 B.C. from their Babylonian captivity, there were enough Psalms to collect and put into a book to be used for worship in the Temple. There were a hundred and fifty in this collection — the same number we have today. Even the personal Psalms took on symbolic meaning, telling of the relation of all Israel to God. They were popular also because they were suited to responsive singing. One part of the congregation would sing one verse and another would sing the next verse.

The Psalms put music into liturgy, which is the proper or technical name for public worship. A modern musician has said that music begins where speech ceases, but in the Psalms music and speech were combined in stirring unison. Many of the Psalms are actually accompanied by directions for singing. In some you will come across the word Selah at the end of a verse. No one knows precisely what this word means, but there is evidence that it had something to do with the way a Psalm was sung. It may well have been written as a kind of pause or rest to emphasize the rhythm. There are times, though, when Selah almost seems to mean Q.E.D. — quod erat demonstrandum, which was to be demonstrated.

Being singable poetry, the Psalms have naturally had a sustained influence on Christian as well as Hebrew worship. In the

Law and the Prophets you had God speaking to man; in the Psalms you have man speaking to and about God and showing an acute awareness of him. St. Augustine, one of the early church-men, thought that the Psalms had a mystical meaning for Christians, although they belonged wholly to the Jewish tradition. The mass of the Roman Catholic Church makes repeated and abundant use of the Psalms, all the more recognizable now that the ritual is in English. And Protestant hymn writers have drawn lavishly upon these ancient verses for inspiration. Isaac Watts, one of the best known, issued a book entitled *The Songs of David Imitated*. You get some measure of his imagination when you find that he once spoke exuberantly of a harp of a thousand strings. Not a few of his hymns are based on the Psalms, perhaps the most notable being "Joy to the World," which was his interpretation of the Ninety-eighth Psalm, reading in part, "Make a joyful noise unto the Lord, all the earth . . . Sing unto the Lord with the harp and the voice of a psalm." There are our words used together and with balance.

In addition to their value as songs of devotion, the Psalms have much to tell us about the sound and beauty of speech. They set pictures to music, make the earth come alive before men's eyes. "Let the sea roar and the fulness thereof. Let the floods clap their hands." The tumult of nature is caught and turned into opera. And the sounds thereof are punctuated by silence. As Elizabeth Barrett Browning wrote, "Then comes the Selah! and the voice is hush'd." There is ebb and flow, rise and fall, quietness and repose along with the shouting. And a man "shall be like a tree planted by rivers of water . . ." Selah.

Q is for Quaker

Q IS FOR QUAKER

Both the letter q and word Quaker are queer. Q might as well be written qu because in the English alphabet q is always followed by u, whether it comes at the beginning or the end of a word. There is no word beginning with q that does not begin with qu, as in quick, quack, quisling, quandary and queasy. And at the end of words, if the q is used, you will find u right along with it, as in antique, physique, unique, and in mystique, recently adopted from the French. Here the letters qu make the sound effect of k. It's an odd arrangement when you come right down to it but it's one you can always count on.

How appropriate, then, that an odd but reliable group of religious people should have a name that begins with Qu. Quaker is a nickname (a sobriquet) but it has stuck for well over three hundred years as a way of referring to those who called themselves Children of Light, Friends in the Truth, plain Friends, and eventually the Religious Society of Friends.

The man whose teaching gave rise to the Friends was

George Fox, a weaver's son apprenticed to a cobbler, who, feeling himself inspired by an inward light, became a lay preacher when he was nineteen. In his Journal Fox noted: "Justice Bennet of Derby was the first that called us Quakers because I did bid them quake and tremble at the word of the Lord."

The name stuck. The word quake comes from old English. Cwacian meant to shake, and those who came in contact with the Quakers were shaken into an awareness of values they had not known before. There was something uncompromising about Fox and his followers. Fox was deeply religious but he refused to have anything to do with the usual ways of expressing his belief. "The Lord showed me, so that I did see clearly," he reported, "that he did not dwell in temples which men had commanded and set up, but in people's hearts. His people were his temple, and he dwelt in them."

The Quakers dealt plainly with all. A Quaker bargain came to mean an offer that had to be accepted or rejected without modification. Friends refused to remove their hats to any man, high or low. The story goes that George Fox once had an audience with King Charles II of England. Fox would not doff his hat and Charles took off his own headgear, saying, "One of us must be uncovered in this presence."

The inward light by which Fox was guided made him no less critical of the state than he was of the church, and he was in and out of prison nine times. His followers were persecuted both in England and in the English Colonies, save for Rhode Island and Pennsylvania, the latter being a colony founded by William Penn, himself a Quaker. Quakers would not bear arms or take oaths. Perhaps most bewildering of all, they granted women rights and dignity and considered them equal to men. And, to compound their audacity, they not only refused to bear arms but also opposed war. They worked in behalf of the downtrodden, seeking reforms in the way prisoners and inmates of insane asylums were treated.

The amazing thing about the Quakers is that they succeeded. They asserted their beliefs and lived them and stuck with them, and still do, so that no religious body is more firmly respected today than the Religious Society of Friends. Except in a few places, they no longer wear conspicuously plain garb, complete with broadbrimmed hats and bonnets that set their men and women apart. And many of them still use thee in writing and speech. But they would be recognized by their founder. By and large, they have been motivated by love and prompted by a desire to give all humanity a chance to live a good life. They put nonviolence into practice centuries before the word got into the language.

Don't thee think we ought to take our hats off to the Quakers? George Fox would say No!

R is for Resipiscence

R IS FOR RESIPISCENCE

You've read, possibly in books dealing with the old West, about men who get religion. Get religion is a strange term but it has a meaning that does not vary. It means that a man has changed. He has been converted, caused to turn around and go in the opposite direction from the one he has been traveling. He may have been a horse thief or a wife-beater or a cusser or a killer. But if he gets religion he becomes a decent and law-abiding citizen who may go so far as to try to make up for some of the mischief and misery he has caused.

One of the things that makes the phrase an odd one is that the word religion appears very few times in the Bible. It's a general word that describes experience from the outside. You speak of the religions of mankind as if you were talking merely about customs. Scholars do not agree on the root of the word. Some say that it comes from the Latin religare, meaning to bind up and to bind together, as a ligament does. Others say that it comes from the Latin relegere, meaning to read and observe again and that religion involves the act of going over something again and again in thought and words.

But, mild as the word is, when we learn that a man has got religion, we know that something explosive and decisive has happened to him. He is no longer the same person, and we know from this fact of change that religion has terrific power, that it can seize a man by the scruff of the neck and teach him to lead a new life.

The elegant word for what takes place when someone gets religion is resipiscence. It is an ugly word in sound but beautiful in meaning. It describes one of the rarest and most profound abilities in the human species, the ability to change one's mind. Change of mind does not happen often but it happens often enough for us to know that it is possible and it has happened often enough to create a word that describes the process. To be sure, the word appears only in the big dictionaries, which means that it is not often needed in ordinary talk.

When applied to religion, resipiscence means more than a change of mind. It means a change for the better. It comes from two Latin words, one meaning to return and the other, sapere, meaning wisdom. The Latin combination resipiscere means literally to come to oneself again. But the key word in the background is sapere. You get wise when you undergo resipiscence — wise to yourself and wise enough to change, and the implication is that the self you left when you went off the track is the better self and you'd better get back to it. It's the real one. As one dictionary puts it, a person is resipiscent if he returns to a sound state of mind.

The classic case of resipiscence is to be found in the story of the Prodigal Son, a parable in which Jesus tells of a young man who took his inheritance and went off into a far country. He spent his money on riotous living and fell so low that the pigs of the farmer he worked for ate better than he did. Then, as an old translation has it, he came to himself. When he did, he acted. He said, "I will arise and go to my father . . ."

He got religion.

S is for Sanctuary

S IS FOR SANCTUARY

And sanctuary is for the birds. So it is in our day, when this ancient and honorable word conjures up a quiet and lovely stretch of woods with muted sounds and tall pillar-like trees that give the place the aspect of a cathedral. There is a hush that is punctuated now and then by some call that may be shrill because it is startling and unexpected, as if a bird felt it owned the place, felt perfectly at home, and you are the intruder.

The idea that fish or fowl or humans should be protected simply because they are present at a certain spot on earth is one of the most appealing ideas in the story of religion. It's particularly appropriate, too, when applied to a wild-life sanctuary because the earliest sacred places in Hebrew history were outdoors; in hills and mountains, on deserts. God was thought of as dwelling in a place and the place where he dwelt was sacred. The word sanctuary derives from sanctus, the Latin word for holy.

Later, houses for God were erected. They were more or less monuments or markers to show that the land round about was holy. And the impression grew that where God dwelt man was protected. He was safe, not only because of the sheltering presence of God but also because goodness was contagious and any man within a sacred place took on certain virtues just by virtue of being there.

Out of this early and deep religious feeling arose the belief that a man ought to be protected in a church or religious house, even though he might have committed a crime. He should have asylum — a word from the Greek, meaning that a person was in a place where those who pursued him did not have the right of seizure. At first Roman law did not recognize the privilege of sanctuary in Christian churches, but it did by the year 399 and by 419 a fugitive was safe if he got within fifty feet of a church door.

Roman monks carried the right to England, and in 600 King Ethelbert made sanctuary a part of his code of laws. He even went so far as to have crosses bearing the word Sanctuarium erected on the highways to guide to the nearest religious house those who stood in need of refuge. There was nothing casual, however, about claiming the protection of a religious house. The code made strict provision for conduct at every point. The fugitive could not stay in sanctuary longer than forty days and then, having confessed his crime to one of the clergy, he had to leave not only sanctuary but also the kingdom. He was given a wooden cross and a white robe to show that he was still under protection and told to get to the nearest port as soon as possible.

In time the system of sanctuary suffered abuse and abomination. Fugitives used religious houses merely as stopovers on the road to escape. Sacred places were desecrated by officers of the state. In 1167 Thomas à Becket, Archbishop of Canterbury and archenemy of Henry II, was murdered by four of Henry's knights at the very altar of Canterbury Cathedral. In 1378 two English squires escaped from the Tower of London and took sanctuary in Westminster Abbey. The King's Council ordered the lieutenant of the Tower to arrest them. The lieutenant, a hot-tempered man, entered the Abbey and seized one. The other was saying mass, but when he resisted arrest, he was killed at the altar.

For all the abuses and the attempts to correct them, the right of sanctuary remained in force among the English until 1623, long enough to establish the belief that religion and protection belong together. Religious ideas passed over into the practices of the state, and as the importance of nations increased, it was embassies rather than churches that often afforded protection.

Sanctuary is still a religious term. It is the name for the most sacred part of a church, the part where the altar stands. In the modern sanctuary, much out of tradition whispers to you, some legend and some fact. Look up at the ceiling of the nave, which is the part of the church that extends between the two main aisles and from the chancel back to the main entrance. Nave comes from the Latin navis, the same word from which we get navy. The ceiling has the shape of the shell of a ship, and it brings to mind the story that some secret worship services of the early Christians were held under upturned boats, affording protection for a forbidden sect. There was protection, to be sure, but there was also the wish to worship. And although the connection between sanctuary and protection has carried the word into every phase of our common life, sanctuary remains a sacred place, a place for worship.

The word worship was spelled worthship until the fourteenth century. In a sacred place men get a feeling of worth.

T is for Tithe

T IS FOR TITHE

One could write a long history of church and state and call it *The
Tithe* and the title would fit. A tithe was once an exaction, something that was demanded, and hence resented. Now it is a gift of
a tenth of one's income for church and welfare work.

Our modern word tithe comes from tethe in Middle English.
Between the years 1050 and 1475, roughly, a tething was a district
where ten families lived. A tethe was a tenth. To tithe means to
give a fixed fraction of all that one receives to help carry on the
Lord's work. The nub of the idea is that the tithe does not belong to you at all. It is something apart from the rest of your
money, as if there were something magic about a tenth.

Is there? There were Ten Commandments and Ten Tribes
of Israel. And an offering of a tenth of the produce of fields and
flocks and even of spoils of war was given by many peoples to
their gods long before tithing was taken up and practiced by the
patriarchs of Israel. The first mentioned in the Scriptures was
that paid by Abraham to the high priest Melchizedek. Later

Jacob promised to pay a tithe for the Lord's aid in various enterprises. In due course the tithe became a part of Mosaic law. Once the tithe was required, trouble commenced. For a man to offer or promise a fraction of his income for good works was one thing. It was quite another to surrender a prescribed part without fail. During some periods of Hebrew history it was necessary to issue stern edicts to keep the practice of tithing alive.

But kept alive it was — on into the days of the New Testament. During the period Jesus taught, the Scribes and Pharisees were so scrupulous that they even set aside a tenth of their garden herbs. Jesus reproached them, saying, "For ye pay tithe of mint and anise and cummin and have omitted the weightier matters of the law, judgment, mercy, and faith." Even so, Jesus did not tell them to stop tithing.

By the time of the Middle Ages tithing was an important means by which the church was supported. In England more than half the income of the church came from the tenth that was required of the populace. The tithe was tantamount to a tax. People had to pay it whether they were believers or not. Church courts enforced a custom that had grown so strong that it had the firmness of law.

The way tithes were collected added to the discomfort of the people, for often they had to be paid in kind. That is, if you had ten bushels of corn, you gave one bushel to the church. There were even tithe-barns set aside to receive the produce when the people delivered it. In some cases every tenth egg was surrendered. The bookkeeping must have been suffocating.

In America there have not been religious taxes since Colonial days. We did not have for long an established church here and, as a consequence, no Disestablishmentarian movement, much less an Antidisestablishmentarian agitation. Among us, giving to religious and humanitarian causes has been voluntary, so the tithe is accepted widely as a good thing. More than a good thing, in fact. During the past two decades ten large Protestant bodies have started campaigns to get their members to tithe. They have succeeded, and in many congregations the amounts contributed have doubled or tripled.

Not only have the results been wonderful for the churches; the effect upon the members who tithe is impressive. Commitment to this form of giving deepens religious experience and makes people feel involved in the program of their church. As one man put it, "You know what you're giving is right. You give until you feel good about it." Volunteer tithers, one churchman says, once started rarely stop. "They are so happy about what happens to them in their own lives that they cling to it."

Many persons who have had the experience go so far as to insist that those who tithe will prosper more than those who don't. They cite cases, including their own. Things just seem to get better. Church leaders admit that improvement in money matters often takes place, but they say that this is not a good reason to tithe. Rather tithing must be approached as a religious act. It links a hallowed custom thousands of years old with modern needs. To pledge and set aside for our fellow man, out of responsible gratitude, a tenth of what comes to us is to recognize at least in a small way that the earth is the Lord's and the fullness thereof.

Th is for Thanksgiving

TH IS FOR THANKSGIVING

If you will look in the big etymological dictionaries, those that give the true or original meaning of words, you will find that the word thank and the word think are closely associated in the languages from which English is derived. In German, for example, the word for thank is danken and the word for think is denken. In Italian the word for thank is grazia and the word that means to think pleasantly is graziare.

Once you discover the similarity, you find it in the small dictionaries as well. Think and thank are alike and, in many cases, if you think, you thank. When you remember the good qualities or deeds of a person, you are likely to feel a sense of gratitude. Of course we can and do make many thoughtless gestures. Yet the closeness of think and thank in many languages suggests an idea we would do well to dwell on. To appreciate means to appraise, to learn the price or value. This requires thought. Thanksgiving at its best is a reflective process.

The United States of America is the only modern country

that has a legally appointed day of national thanksgiving. And this day is not much more than a hundred years old, having been instituted by President Abraham Lincoln in 1863. George Washington had proclaimed thanksgiving as a national duty in the year of his inauguration — 1789. Various states issued proclamations after that, and in 1859 thirty states held thanksgiving festivals on the same day. But there was no occasion for giving thanks in unison until Lincoln appointed the last Thursday of November as a time when the gifts of God should be acknowledged "with one heart and one voice by the whole American people."

A national day of thanks had been repeatedly urged by Mrs. Sarah Josepha Hale through her editorials in *Godey's Lady's Book*, the most widely circulated magazine of the day. A month before Lincoln acted she asked: "In a time of national darkness and sore troubles shall we not recognize that the goodness of God never faileth?"

Lincoln responded to the spirit of her plea. His proclamation was issued at the darkest hour of the Republic. The nation was divided by a bloody war. That year one battle, at Gettysburg, had left forty-three thousand dead and wounded. Draft riots had broken out in New York City, where a thousand persons had been killed or hurt and fires had destroyed residences, hotels, restaurants and public buildings. The prospect of an American future could not have been more obscured by gloom.

Yet it was at this moment that Lincoln asked the American people to give thanks. Anybody can be grateful if all goes well and the table and stomach are full. But thanksgiving becomes us and ennobles us when it is separated from good fortune. It may be intensified by a feeling of luck but it ought not to depend on it. It comes from reflection, from assessment, from appreciation.

And a sense of thanks is kept alive and encouraged by the reminders of religion. Mrs. Hale cited as precedent for the holiday she urged the harvest festivals of the Jews, based on the injunction: "Neither be ye sorry, for the joy of the Lord is your strength." The earliest Thanksgiving Day on American shores grew out of devotion. It took place in 1621 among the Pilgrims at Plymouth. Established here ten years before the stern Puritans came, the Pilgrims were a gentle and devout people and the feast they held to celebrate the fruits of the harvest that first year they shared with the neighboring Indians.

Thanksgiving is a part of every service of worship, an informal and inescapable part even if it is not worked into the ritual. I remember the thrill I had in a church made up of Afro-American members when I heard the preacher thank God in prayer for waking up that morning and "finding the blood coursing through my body." He was thinking.

So was the man who wrote the prayer known as A General Thanksgiving. It is said to have been based on a private prayer of Elizabeth I and was composed by Bishop Edward Reynolds of Norwich, England, in the form now used, appearing first in the *Book of Common Prayer* of the Church of England in 1662. When the Prayer Book was revised and adopted by the Protestant Episcopal Church in the United States after the Revolution, it was not only kept but moved from occasional prayers and made a regular part of morning worship. For years it was read by the minister alone and then it was appointed to be read by minister and congregation together. There are in it passages of great beauty to express the highest feelings of all:

... We beseech thee, give us that due sense of all thy mercies, that our hearts may be unfeignedly thankful; and that we may show forth thy praise, not only with our lips, but in our lives, by giving up ourselves to thy service ...

U is for Unction

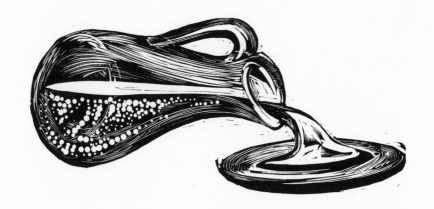

U IS FOR UNCTION

In newspapers we read now and then that a person who is quite ill and not expected to live has been given Extreme Unction. The case usually appears hopeless and the impression gained is that the ceremony, usually referred to as the last rites, is performed to prepare the soul for death. But the word extreme means last only in that Extreme Unction is the last of the listed anointings authorized by the Roman Catholic Church. It is not a desperate measure but a sacrament. It is done with the oil of the sick specially blessed and in the hope that the person who receives the sacrament may be restored to health. It is given only to persons whose lives are feared of because of sickness or injury — not to men going into battle, for example, or to persons who are about to undergo an operation.

Unction is simply the ceremony of anointing with oil and it is one of the longest continued practices in the Judeo-Christian tradition. Among the Jews in olden times men were anointed, as in the case of Samuel's anointing Saul as the first king of Israel.

The Temple was anointed, as were the furnishings in it, and the animals to be sacrificed. The oil of unction used in Hebrew ceremonies was olive oil, greatly refined for religious purposes, and combined with balsam and myrrh and other fragrant ingredients. Strict rules were laid down for its preparation. It was carefully preserved for use on high occasions, to be poured out upon people or things as a symbol of special benediction. Among the blessings cited by the singer of the Twenty-third Psalm is that of the Lord's anointing his head with oil.

Unction passed logically into Christian practice. The very language used to describe the central figure of the new faith was a sign and token of the old Hebraic heritage. Christ is the English form of the Greek word Christos, which means The Anointed One.

As a word, unction has significance that goes far beyond the act of anointing. Hence its origin cannot but seem to us quite lowly, not to say inelegant. It comes from the Latin ungere: to smear. Unction and anoint are from the same root. Not through origin but through religious association these words have acquired dignity. Anoint has a beauty of sound; it falls well upon the ear. To many unction is an appealing word. Justice Oliver Wendell Holmes once spoke of a man who was "doing his work with pleasant unction." The words were coming smoothly. And you will read that powerful preachers of an early day spoke with unction. They had fluency, having been anointed with power from on high.

But if unction is good as a noun, the adjective unctuous is rarely used in a favorable sense — at least not when applied to people. It can be used to describe soil that is soft or rich or adhesive. Nathaniel Hawthorne speaks beautifully of "oak, now black with time and unctuous with kitchen smoke." It may be all right for things to be unctuous but it is not all right for a person. One who is said to be unctuous in speech or manner has a kind of oily piety. He is slippery, like boiled okra, and you can't quite trust or place him. He is, to borrow a line from Bergen Evans, "a little more than *smooth,* a little less than *greasy.*"

Unction may have a varied and dubious appeal because of its association with unctuous, but its lay brother, unguent, has been in good repute since it was introduced around 1440. Unguent has sales appeal, being the base word of a modern commercial product, Unguentine. And ointment, which is virtually the same word as unguent, has such a gentle sound that it soothes one to say it.

Unguent is a case where a religious term in modified form has got over into common parlance and appeals to all, saint and sinner alike. Yet you wonder what appeal unguents and ointments would have to our minds if unction had not had such a long-standing religious history. Do words work their way into the psyche? Both ointment and unguent are intended to benefit and to heal.

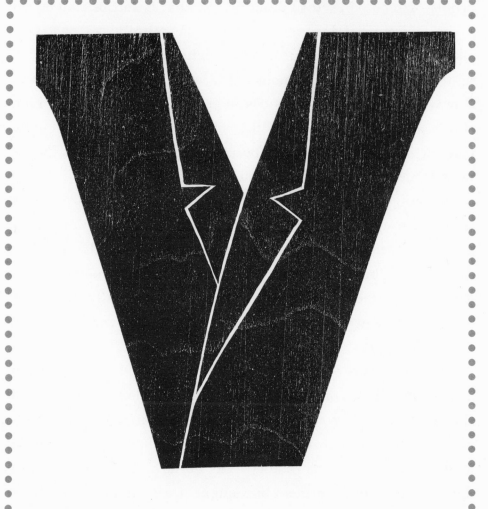

V is for Vestments

V IS FOR VESTMENTS

The clothes worn in religious ceremonies are vestments, a word that comes from the Latin vestis. You find vestis turning up in all sorts of strange places, and every place it turns up it points up the importance of attire. You find it in the English word vest, a short garment that comes only to the waist and is logically called a waistcoat by the British. You get it also in words that show the idealized meaning of special clothes, as in the word invest, where you are given attire suited to your position or role; in divest, where you are deprived of the authority given you by robes of office. And you get it in the word travesty, which means that something is dressed against the appropriate role.

You have heard of vested interests. It's a term popular with politicians and professors. It means interests clothed in rights thought to be of long standing, and to belong to one because of his position. If your interest is vested it wears the robes appropriate to your status. In law it means that your right is absolute.

It is fitting that the word vestment should come out of the

Roman manner of speech, for it is from practices of the Roman Catholic Church that a great many of our ceremonial robes take their form and etiquette. To be sure, robes of priestly office are much older, having been prescribed in detail to Moses, even to the colors, which were to be gold, violet, purple and scarlet. But the robes worn today in both the Roman and Anglican services are distinct from those of the Old Testament, dating from the days when Christians became acceptable in Rome. They set aside their best suits, their Sunday-go-to-meeting clothes, for service at the altar. The attire of upper-class Romans, arrayed in their Sunday best, became in time the vesture of priests and dignitaries of the church.

Religion is a pageant, often a beautiful one. It is much more, but almost all religious ceremonies of almost all faiths involve acting a role, with men and women costumed for the parts. In some Protestant groups the acting and the robing are kept to a minimum, but worshipers bow or kneel to pray or stand to sing or show in some way that they are not their street selves but engaged in acts that symbolize what they feel. In most churches the choir is robed and often marches into the church. The minister may wear a gown of a sort different from the choir to set him apart and show that he has a separate function. Even in the simplest services you get a hint of pageantry and parade, and of course in elaborate observances you get what amounts to pomp, from the Greek word for procession.

Clothes played such an important part in services of worship that a room or part of a church was set aside to hold the vestments. It was called a vestiary at first and then a vestry. In the

Church of England those who managed the business of the local parish met periodically in the vestry and came to be called vestrymen. The term carried over into English colonies and later into the Protestant Episcopal Church. The office has dignity and Episcopalians understand its importance. But outsiders will now and then ask a vestryman if he looks after vestments. He doesn't. It's another one of those cases where the meaning of a word harks back to remote association. Officials who manage the local business of Methodist churches, for example, are called stewards. In Old English a steward was a sty ward or guard, a man who tended an enclosure for swine or other small animals. Later he grew in grace and managed larger matters and the spelling was changed slightly. So don't get the impression that a Methodist steward looks after a pig sty any more than a vestryman takes care of vestments.

W is for Whitsuntide

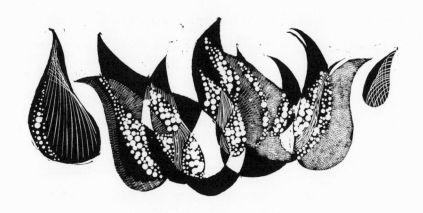

W IS FOR WHITSUNTIDE

White Sunday is the seventh Sunday following Easter. Whitsuntide is the name given the week (and chiefly the first three days) following Whitsunday.

Pentecost, a high holy day of the Hebrew faith, falls on the same day as Whitsunday. The word Pentecost comes from the Greek word for fiftieth day it tells us that Pentecost is fifty days from the time of the feast of the Passover.

So we have the remarkable fact that Judaism and Christianity celebrate the same birthday. Pentecost calls back to mind the event of the delivery of the Ten Commandments to Moses on Mount Sinai. It was these laws that set the Hebrews apart as a people and called them into being as a nation.

Among Christians Whitsunday marks the time when special and overwhelming blessings fell upon and awakened the Disciples after the resurrection of Christ. The day of Pentecost was the beginning of the Christian Church. Both the events celebrated by Pentecost in the Jewish faith and by Whitsunday in the Christian calendar were attended by fire. The record in the Old Testament tells us that Mount Sinai was aflame when Moses received the Ten Commandments and that the fire was a manifestation of God, a sure sign of his presence. And Pentecost is spoken of among the more zealous Christians as the time when the fire fell. A modern translation of the New Testament describes the scene: "And there appeared to them tongues like flames of fire, dispersed among them and resting on each one." A white light surrounded the events and lit up the faces of the believers. It was a time of incandescence, the word coming from the Latin to designate heat so intense that it produces a white light.

What happened at the first Christian Pentecost, according to New Testament accounts, was the result of a gift. The blessing came unbidden. The Greek word for gift or favor is charisma. This is a word that has long slept in the dictionaries. It was used, but rarely, in religious circles and then to describe an extraordinary ability to heal or to do good for others. By degrees it came to be applied to people who had exceptional influence over other people, a kind of magnetic power. In our day the word was suddenly discovered, as if for the first time, and has come to be used in all sorts of ways. Not long ago a picture magazine came out with a story headed: NEW CHARISMA FOR CHICAGO.

In a strange way, then, the word charisma is transferred from its original meaning to an acquired meaning and it is tied up with illumination, with an aura of brightness, with having a glow, being turned on. Light accompanies great events in religious history and surrounds great personages in the story of religion. A nimbus or halo around holy figures in paintings is a token of the link between light and sanctity. When Jesus took Peter, James and John into a high mountain to pray, the account says that Jesus was "transfigured before them: and his face did shine as the sun, and his raiment was white as light."

This sense of blinding light runs right on through and carries over into the traditions that treat of Christian faith. It appears brilliantly in the story of the Holy Grail, the cup or chalice which, according to the Arthurian legend, was used at the Last Supper. It was said to be visible only to those who were morally and spiritually worthy. One day the Holy Grail came to Camelot. King Arthur and his knights had gone into the great hall and had taken their appointed places at the Round Table.

"Then on a sudden a sunbeam cut through the gloom from end to end of the great hall, seven times more clear than ever man saw on the brightest day of summer; and the glory of God was upon them all. Then the Holy Grail entered into the hall covered in a cloth of white Samite, so filled with glorious light that none could behold it."

Some realists say that Whitsunday, a name English in origin, is so called because of the white garments worn at Pentecost by the newly baptized. The day before Easter was once the time of a great baptismal ceremony, but the English weather was so unfriendly at the Easter season that the ceremony was put off seven weeks until Pentecost, when it was likely to be warmer. Anyone who knows the English climate will find the theory plausible. But others prefer to think that Whitsunday bespeaks the radiance of persons under the spell of a profound experience. We do know that this radiance occurs and that there ought to be a time set aside to celebrate it.

X is for Christmas

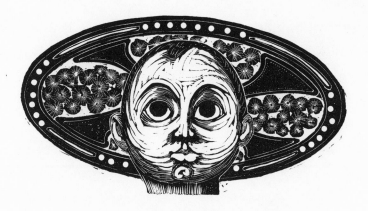

X IS FOR CHRISTMAS

And many would say, what a pity! Xmas as a word looks bob-tailed, truncated, careless at best. Yet X *is* for Christmas. For more than four hundred years this way of writing Christmas has been in honored use, and the fact that the form survives and is still used tells a great deal about both language and custom.

The X in Xmas is not, as some people assume, a stroke of abbreviation, nor yet a sign of the cross. Rather it is the Roman way of writing the Greek letter chi, which is the first letter in the spelling of Christos. Sometimes you may see a combination of the first and second letters in Christos — chi and rho — used as a liturgical or decorative symbol. This is called a Christo-gram. To get Christmas you add the word mass to Christ and you have the Feast of the Nativity, celebrating Christ's birth. Or, if you prefer the Roman to the Greek, you spell it Xmas.

Latin prevailed in England before English; Latin was Roman and Christmas had strong Roman ties. How December 25 was chosen as the date for Christmas, no one knows, but the date was close to the feast of Saturnalia which the Romans had celebrated with jubilation and tempestuous revelry, and historians think that the Feast of the Nativity was instituted to counter or rival the Roman holiday. Possibly so, but if so, the scheme didn't work. Certainly not at first. A spirit of pagan gaiety marked Christmas from its beginnings, and only gradually and only in certain countries and places did rites and ceremonies take over and lend some religious dignity to the occasion.

The rivalry between the Christ mass and Saturnalia persisted and persists. But setting up the Feast of the Nativity, which was observed as early as the days of Constantine, did ring a change. It helped to turn the Christian mind from death to birth. The early church honored the death of martyrs, calling the time of their death their "birthdays in eternity." In a like manner the ceremonies of the church stressed the crucifixion and resurrection. By the fourth century, however, there began commemorations of the life of Christ and his mother and some efforts were made to make the birth of Christ important if not central in church ceremony. The cradle as well as the cross became a symbol of the Christ.

Meanwhile the idea of Christmas as a time of merriment grew in popularity — and it continued to grow, offering a festival that combined pagan gaiety with religious solemnity. The Germans and Scandinavians in particular were hearty Christmas people and developed many customs that had little to do with the Nativity. Nor did those of the English in the early days. Sir Walter Scott wrote: "A Christmas gambol could often cheer/ The poor man's heart through half the year."

In time the United States of America became the great

Roman Christmas country, what with customs from many lands brought by immigrants, giving us a kind of world and worldly Christmas. It is said that the Hessians during the War of the Revolution were the first to introduce Christmas trees among us. Being as a people given to exaggeration, we went whole hog on what we adopted, erecting a Christmas tree sixty-five feet high and festooned with a thousand lights. We have surrounded Christmas with the gaudiest possible displays, so that one friend of mine looked out over the Boston Common at the lights and decorations and had only one word to describe the scene: Christtorama.

During the centuries protests aplenty have been made against frivolity as the essential element of Christmas. Some of these protests have been pretty strenuous. Puritan England's Long Parliament in 1644 passed ordinances against Christmas. In the American colonies both the Puritans and the Pilgrims disdained the day. Along with the protests, and independent of them, there has grown up a gradual movement toward making Christmas religious. More and more oratorios, hymns, songs, special prayers and sermons and services of public worship help to stress the cradle theme. The fact that Advent now culminates at and in Christmas helps to underline Christmas as a time of birth and beginning and as a tremendous moment in a religion based on love and nurture and tenderness.

Christmas is still a day with much of its meaning hidden in history and trappings. In mathematics X stands for the unknown quantity. So we might say in this respect also that X is for Christmas. It's up to us to find the unknown quantity.

Y is for Yahweh

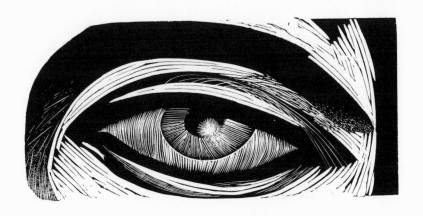

Y IS FOR YAHWEH

The Greek heavens were peopled with gods and goddesses and godlets, all quite human in their doings and gaddings, coming down to earth and going back to Olympus, Yo-Yo fashion, making trouble among humans when they were not getting into mischief themselves. The story of Echo, who started out as a beautiful nymph, gives you an idea of what went on. The great god Zeus often came down to pay court to a covey of nymphs, much to the displeasure of his wife Hera, who tried not to let him out of her sight. Zeus appointed Echo to engage Hera in conversation so charmingly that she would be diverted and not know what he was up to. Hera eventually caught on to the trick and she was so mortified and enraged that she condemned Echo to wander over the earth and never speak unless she was spoken to — and then only to repeat what had been said to her. It was harsh punishment for a good talker.

At first the Hebrews also had many gods in many places and with many names. But the Hebrew idea of the Deity grew. It did not remain fixed, as did the cast of the Greek gods. The Hebrew idea evolved toward monotheism, or belief in one God, and then there were many names to describe various attributes of the same being. The name of the deity who created the heavens and earth as recorded in Genesis was Elohim, and it is thought to come from a Hebrew word meaning to be strong or mighty. It could apply to the gods of other peoples, as, for example, to Astarte, the goddess of the Zidonians.

Then, as Hebrew faith grew more devout and complex, there came a name for their One God that they shared with no religion and applied to no other deity. It was a name that became more sacred as time went on until it got to a point where it could not be uttered by ordinary Jews at all. It was not to be taken in vain. To speak it was to blaspheme. When one Jew "thought another Jew had unlawfully uttered the sacred Name, he must rend his clothes, that being a symbol of rejection and also the common sign of mourning."

The sacred name was revealed to Moses after he had escaped from Egypt and had married one of the daughters of Jethro, the high priest of Midian. One day when he kept the flock of Jethro his father-in-law in a remote part of the land near Sinai the Lord appeared to him out of the burning bush and told him that the time had come to deliver the Children of Israel from bondage in the land of Egypt. Moses was overcome at the prospect of the task but agreed — with some reluctance — and then he asked the Voice what name he should use when he told the Children of Israel of the plan for their deliverance.

"And God said unto Moses, I AM THAT I AM: and he said,

Thus shalt thou say unto the children of Israel, I AM hath sent me unto you."

It was a new name for God, one that had not been known to Abraham, Isaac, or Jacob. There was more to God now than strength and power as shown in fire and wind. Those elements of strength remained and would still be a part of His manifestation, but the fresh sense of God revealed to Moses showed that He was also above and beyond, that He was not to be confined to little forms and names men had given Him in the past. For the name given Him now derived from the Hebrew verb meaning to be. God spoke to Moses in the first person and gave the name I AM. Others would use the third person, HE IS.

This God could not be easily comprehended, as might Zeus in pursuit of nymphs. He could not be dragged into casual speech. The high priest in the Temple might pronounce the Name, but in the synagogue, which was the place where the common people worshiped, another word for God was used. Because Hebrew was written without vowels, the sacred Name appeared in sacred literature simply as JHVH, a form known in Greek translation as the Tetragrammaton — from tetra, meaning four and gramma, meaning letter. No wonder Christian theologians decided around the year 1520 to take vowels from Adhonai, a lesser word for God, and make the word Jehovah. The result was a convenience in reading, but the word Jehovah is only a faint and wandering echo of the great I AM.

Our English word God is of Middle English and Anglo-Saxon origin. It derivation is uncertain but it seems to have come from a verb meaning to invoke. It is a casual or at least flexible word and our reverence for it is determined largely by our mood or the tone of voice in which the name is said or the circumstances in which we hear it. Like the early Hebrews, we have many other names: the Almighty, the Supreme Being, Cosmic Force, First Cause. These names acknowledge the complexity and mystery of the universe and they remind us in an age of know-it-all that, notwithstanding man's achievements and penetration, there is something not immediately understandable.

It is Yahweh: I AM.

Z is for Zion

Z IS FOR ZION

Have you ever been told you were making a mountain out of a molehill? Usually it means to take a trifle and blow it up out of all proportion to its importance. The story of Zion, however, is a true story of taking a hill and making a mountain out of it. Zion originally was only the name of one of the seven hills on which Jerusalem was built. Before David took the hill by stealth near the year 1000 B.C. it was a fortified eminence under the control of the Jebusites, an Egyptian tribe. Then David established his residence there as the second king of Israel and the hill became Mount Zion, a more dignified term. David made Jerusalem his capital, and the word Zion came to designate the whole city. Jerusalem was Zion. In time it came to represent all of Israel and the essence of the Hebrew religion, gaining height through David's reign and even more under his son, Solomon, who built a temple there from cedars of Lebanon, the royal palace, other buildings, and then a wall around the city.

Zion thus grew to be the symbolic and sentimental name

for the aspirations of Israel. It was a summary word, short, and easy to work into Psalms. It was a memory word, full of nostalgia in times of trial, as when the Jews were taken into captivity: "By the rivers of Babylon, there we sat down, yea, we wept, when we remembered Zion." The Psalmist goes on: "They that carried us away captive required of us a song; and they that wasted us required of us mirth, saying, sing us one of the songs of Zion." There had been gaiety in Israel. The answer to the Babylonians is given in the lament of the verse, "How shall we sing the Lord's song in a strange land?"

Not only did Zion become the key word in the life and history of the Jews, it also became an exalted term in Christianity, notably among Protestant bodies. Those who wrote Christian hymns took Judaic terms and gave them Christian meaning, folding them into the Christian faith and order of service. Isaac Watts, who lived about the time of William Penn, wrote a number of hymns designed to make the Psalms suited to Protestant worship. He wanted "to make David speak like a Christian."

Zion, along with other words such as Beulah Land, acquired a meaning distinctly Christian, as if it had not been used by the Hebrews. It became a name for the Christian heaven. One of the most stirring songs expressing this belief is entitled "We're Marching to Zion." The words are put to a metrical, spirited tune with a strong beat, so that if you have not heard it you can imagine the giddap of the chorus: "We're Marching to Zion,/ Beautiful, beautiful Zion./We're marching upward to Zion-on-on-nnn,/The beautiful City of God." You don't sing it or hear it without marching standing still.

In the poetry of faith Zion no longer belongs to the Jews alone. It stands for an ideal shared by Jews and Christians alike, an ideal far from realized, much less attained. The name of a hill in Jerusalem has become a word of many colors held in common by many faiths and shades of belief. To all it conjures up a memory or sets a goal for the imagination.

The gamut of human aspiration, the whole range of it, can be found in the Bible — from Genesis to Revelation, from the first stirrings of life to its zenith, from Alpha to Omega, and the concept of Zion is the climax. The summary of it is to be found in the latest translation of the twenty-first chapter of the Book of Revelation, which reads in part:

"Then I saw a new heaven and a new earth. And I saw the Holy City, the new Jerusalem, coming down out of heaven from God. I heard a loud voice speaking from the throne: 'Now God's home is with men! He will live with them and they shall be his people. He will wipe all tears from their eyes. There will be no more death, no more grief, crying, or pain.'"

When we consider the ideal and the dream, we cannot but hope that we're all marching to Zion.

PERSONAL

Some of my best friends are a thousand years old — and more. They are scholars who have searched the records and collated data on religious words and the emotions connected with them. If scholars and scribes had not done the grubbing, this book would have been impossible to compile. Hence I must now bow in the direction of the ages past and of reference books present.

And, of course, some of my sources are live. People provide the inspiration that makes reference material breathe. The source of the idea that led to the book was a person. Elizabeth Atkinson Plaisted, who worked with me on *The Abecedarian Book*, suggested that there ought to be an alphabet book of religious terms called *A Is for Advent*. The suggestion stirred my curiosity until it turned into wonder, and the more we read and searched the greater became the lure of the neglected and of the poorly understood.

Many others helped as the work progressed, and the eagerness with which friends volunteered and leaped in to help was a tribute not only to their good nature but also, I thought, to the vitality and appeal of the idea. Mr. and Mrs. Jac Austin (to take a collective example) spent hours drawing up a word list from which selections might ultimately be made. Mrs. Larry Collins, grounded in basic terms of devotion through teaching in church school, sent me essays and comments on words growing out of religious practices. Ruth Sheldon Knowles turned up good references on manna and on the protein manna that may come from oil. Caroline Rogers, who has an omnivorous eye, collected many items to show how religious terms have been used in literature, keeping faithfully alert to the growing content of the book in all the reading she did.

Persons who read the manuscript while it was in preparation proved to be excellent sources. Dr. Norman Temme of The American Bible Society heartened me by the patience and care with which he pored over what I had written. He made important corrections but is hereby absolved from responsibility for any errors that remain. What pleased me most, however, was the fact that he was led to turn up and send me from his files material which he knew would round out various chapters and lend the book as a whole greater interest.

Paul R. Reynolds gave the book a good going over for inconsistencies. Sidney Gordon read the manuscript from a cultured British point of view and caught me up on several points, objecting, for instance, to my reference to Charles II as the playboy king of England. I took it out but I still rather like it. Eva H. Grant, a skilled and expert worker with both copy and ideas, detected slips and discrepancies that made further study necessary. Genevieve Egerton, fully versed in historical research, made detailed comments on an early draft. Ann Yeager Barnes offered chastening observations on passages that needed reworking.

So it goes until the conscience aches in retrospect, lest someone be overlooked. It's like one of those church suppers at which the chairman names all the persons to be thanked and forgets to mention the cooks. The equitable distribution of acknowledgments is a task beyond any author and, even now, I wonder how many indirect contributors I have neglected when I suddenly recall that it was the interest Elizabeth Turnbull took in the Tetragrammaton that led to the choice of Yahweh for Y.

I suppose the moral is that anyone who starts out to find the depth of a word is bound to realize how much help can be had from friends and acquaintances as well as from books. If you don't believe it, try during the next month to see what you can discover — and from what sources — about the origin and derivation and current use of one of the many words I reluctantly omitted from this book:

Glossolalia.

This book is illuminated with original
woodcuts and engravings
by Corinne and Robert Borja.

It was set in 12 point Bookman by Wrightson
Typographers, printed by offset at Halliday
Lithograph Corp. on 70 lb. Warren's 1854
regular offset and bound at Quinn & Boden

Books by Charles W. Ferguson

Naked to Mine Enemies: The Life of Cardinal Wolsey

Say It with Words

Getting to Know the U.S.A.

The Abecedarian Book

The Male Attitude

A Is for Advent